Swift Translation Guide for Objective-C Developers

DEVELOP AND DESIGN

Maurice Kelly

PEACHPIT PRESS
WWW.PEACHPIT.COM

Swift Translation Guide for Objective-C Developers: Develop and Design
Maurice Kelly

Peachpit Press

www.peachpit.com
To report errors, please send a note to errata@peachpit.com

Peachpit Press is a division of Pearson Education.

Editor: Robyn G. Thomas
Copyeditor: Darren Meiss
Proofreader: Nancy Bell
Technical editor: Mark Goody
Compositor: Danielle Foster
Indexer: Valerie Haynes Perry
Cover design: Aren Straiger
Interior design: Mimi Heft

Notice of Rights

Notice of Liability

Trademarks

ISBN-13: 978-0-134-04469-9
ISBN-10:   0-134-04469-X

9 8 7 6 5 4 3 2 1

Printed and bound in the United States of America

Once more, I couldn't have completed this project without the support, encouragement, and love of my wife, Fiona, and our wonderful girls, Aoibhínn and Caoimhe. "Mank ooo" for giving me lots of smiles and hugs every time I finished writing.

To my parents, brother, sister, and our extended families— thanks for looking interested when I talked about Swift, and for putting up with all the excuses that began with "But I'm working on the book…"

ACKNOWLEDGMENTS

I would like to thank the engineering management chain at my employers, ShopKeep Inc., particularly Stepan Hruda, Duncan Grazier, Jason Ordway, and Miriam Kerbache. They supported this endeavor by giving me the permission and space to work on it, and by giving me an enjoyable and progressive engineering environment to return to.

Mark Goody deserves thanks on many levels for his help with this book: As a friend, technical editor, and oft-inspirator, it feels wrong to boil it down to just one word, but all I can say is thanks.

It was a pleasure to work again with Robyn Thomas on this book. Robyn puts up with my poor language skills, despite the constant ribbing about U.S. English, and for that she is forgiven for her predilection toward z, and aversion to u. Thanks also to Clifford Colby for the wonderful lunch in San Francisco and for taking a chance on me with another book. I hope to buy you lunch in return sometime.

ABOUT THE AUTHOR

Maurice Kelly has been engineering software since leaving university in 2001. After spending many years working on server software for mobile telecoms, he took a change of direction to work at the user-facing end by becoming an iOS developer. He has a love for synthesizers and music, and dreams of owning a Land Rover Defender someday. He lives with his wife and children just outside Dromara, a small village in Northern Ireland.

CONTENTS

INTRODUCTION

When Apple introduced Swift at the Apple WWDC (Worldwide Developers Conference) in 2014, the audience, packed full of developers for the Apple platforms, was stunned and silent. Swift is the first truly new programming language to be introduced for the Mac development platform in its history; Objective-C, C++, and C were all existing languages. Swift was built from the ground up, by Apple and for Apple.

Apple described the new Swift language as "Objective-C without the C," but that doesn't really do it justice. Swift is more of a completely new programming language than simply Objective-C with the C heritage extracted.

A HISTORY

For many Apple-centric developers, especially those developing for the iOS platform, the introduction of a new language is a seismic change. Objective-C has been our go-to programming language for years, and it often feels like it has been the only language we have ever used. Yet it wasn't always that way...

While Objective-C has existed since the 1980s, it wasn't adopted for Mac OS development until after the acquisition of NeXT, a company founded by Steve Jobs in the mid-80s, by Apple in 1996. NeXT had selected Objective-C as the primary programming language for its NeXTSTEP operating system. NeXTSTEP was a major influence on the development of Mac OS X, and it was perhaps inevitable that Objective-C would come to be a dominant language in the OS X ecosystem.

Before the acquisition of NeXT, a number of different languages were popularly used to develop Mac applications. Early Mac developers commonly used Pascal to write their apps, and Apple would later introduce Object Pascal as an object-oriented extension of the language.

When Mac hardware switched from 68K to PowerPC, Apple took the opportunity to adopt C++ and rewrite its MacApp framework. Prior to the NeXT acquisition, most Mac applications were written in C++. The adoption of NeXTSTEP, and its Objective-C-based frameworks, as the foundation for Mac OS X would have been a serious bump in the road, because developers would have needed to re-implement their applications in Objective-C.

Thankfully, Apple introduced not just the Cocoa framework, which of course was based on Objective-C, but also a peer framework named Carbon that was programmed in C++. This offered existing developers a smoother path to porting their classic Mac OS apps to Mac OS X. Though Carbon has been deprecated for a number of years, it existed for quite some time, so it is fair to say that C++ was a very popular language for OS X development alongside Objective-C and not just before it. Even today, C++ is still available to use in Xcode as both a pure language and as Objective-C++. Maybe it is not surprising that in many ways Swift has many C++ "flavors" to it, such as overloading and generics.

Despite being introduced as "Objective-C without the C," Swift is still very much a member of the extended C family of languages. As a result, it should still feel somewhat familiar to developers coming from C, C++, and Java, and especially to developers coming from Objective-C.

HOW TO USE THIS BOOK

This is not a traditional technical book for a new programming language: This is a translation guide, with an express purpose of helping existing developers of OS X and iOS applications in Objective-C migrate their skill sets to the new language.

HOW YOU WILL LEARN

We begin by examining the core constructs of the Objective-C language, picking apart its syntax, and showing you how it differs from Swift. The book focuses mainly on short samples of code from both languages, illustrating how the syntax of Objective-C translates to Swift. The languages are interspersed, and you'll find labels in the margins to help you quickly distinguish between Objective-C and Swift code.

```
[greetingMaker produceGreeting:^NSString *(NSString *format, NSString *name) {    Objective-C
    return [NSString stringWithFormat:format, name];
}];
```

```
greetingMaker.produceGreeting( { (format: String, name: String) -> (String) in    Swift
    return NSString(format:format, name)
} )
```

You'll also find notes containing additional information about the topics.

> **NOTE:** Properties must always be declared as var in the protocol, even if you do not intend to use them as a variable in the conforming type. When you implement a protocol, you are free to redefine the property as a constant if you wish.

Swift and Xcode 6 present a completely new way to experiment with code in the form of Swift playgrounds. The examples in this book are as short as possible so you can type them into a Swift playground in order to see the results, and to modify the code for the purposes of experimentation. Most of the code examples are collated into Swift playground files and available for download at the website to accompany the book at http://swift-translation.guide.

WHAT YOU WILL LEARN

This book takes the existing syntax, constructs, and patterns from Objective-C and shows how they can be translated into Swift. We'll strive to point out potential pitfalls along the way, highlight shortcomings of the new language, and illustrate new ways of doing things that were never before possible in Objective-C.

This book assumes that you are familiar with Apple's Foundation, Cocoa, and/or CocoaTouch frameworks. Although the programming language may be changing, these frameworks make developing for OS X and iOS such a rich experience and will largely remain the same.

At the time of this writing, Swift was at version 1.1 but the language is evolving rapidly. If you have any problems with the code samples, please look in the online documentation for the standard library (bit.ly/apple-swift-docs) to check that the syntax is actually the latest.

WELCOME TO SWIFT

You most likely have the tools you need already installed to develop your iOS or OS X apps in Swift rather than Objective-C. For iOS apps, you need at least Xcode 6.0; for OS X development, you need at least Xcode 6.1. If you're not running the right version, upgrade using the Mac App Store, or download a version from the Apple Developer Center at http://developer.apple.com.

SWIFT'S GOALS

When introducing Swift to the world, Apple had three goals for the new language: It had to be safe, modern, and powerful.

SAFE

Swift added and removed programming concepts to make it a safer language than Objective-C. In the new additions column are optional variables, constant references, and numerous syntactical changes that reduce the scope for programming logic errors. Under removals, say goodbye to pointers and the ability to send messages to nil objects.

MODERN

Swift is a decidedly more modern language than Objective-C. Functions are treated as first class types, generics provide a more extensible base for custom collections, and even subtle changes like type inference can leave Objective-C looking increasingly dated. Structures and enumerations have been overhauled, taking them from their humble C origins and making them an alternative to classes for many data needs.

POWERFUL

Apple has made bold claims about Swift's performance in comparison to Objective-C and other high-level languages, some of which appear to be starting to hold water in real-world tests. Swift has a powerful feature set and syntax, which allow iOS and OS X developers to do more than they ever have before.

NEW TOOLS

Xcode 6 comes with a pair of new tools to help you experiment with Swift: playgrounds and the REPL.

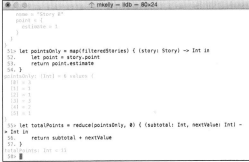

PLAYGROUNDS

Swift playgrounds bring a new way of experimentation to Xcode.

Playgrounds are interactive sandbox documents in which you can experiment with Swift's new ideas without worrying about creating new projects or dirtying your existing projects. They can work with text, images, or even complex SpriteKit animations.

REPL

The Swift REPL allows interactive programming from a command-line interface.

A Read-Eval-Print-Loop (REPL) tool gives you access to a playground-like environment from the command line. They are a great way to test syntax or a new idea quickly, without the overhead of having to run Xcode.

CHAPTER 1
Creating Swift Projects

Getting started with Swift development is simple if you are already an iOS or OS X developer. The entire Swift toolchain is supplied with Xcode 6 and even comes with a few extra goodies, such as the Swift REPL and playgrounds.

YOUR FIRST SWIFT PROJECT

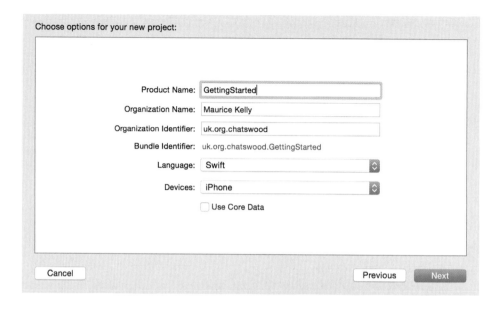

To create your first Swift project, choose File > New > Project from the main menu. Xcode displays the template chooser dialog allowing you to select the type of iOS or OS X project you want to create—a single view iOS application is sufficient to follow along. The "Choose options for your new project" dialog looks very similar to the way it did in previous Xcode versions, with two significant differences: The Class Prefix field is no longer present and has been replaced with a Language pop-up menu (**Figure 1.1**).

The Language pop-up menu is the key to creating a Swift project—clicking it presents you with two options: Swift and Objective-C. Choose Swift, fill in your remaining details, and click Next to finish creating the project as you normally would. And that's it. The next phase of your development career has begun.

FUNDAMENTAL DIFFERENCES

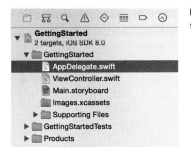

FIGURE 1.2 A slightly sparser project navigator

On first glance, your newly created project should look similar to those you created for Objective-C. A closer look at the folder structure in the project navigator (**Figure 1.2**) reveals some fundamental differences between Swift and Objective-C.

NO MORE HEADER FILES

The first difference is that there are no header files—each Swift compilation unit consists of a single file with a `.swift` extension. Although many compilation units will be classes, creating `.swift` files that contain stand-alone functions, structures, enumerations, and more is valid.

Without a header file, how do you import a class or some other data type for use in your own class? Swift does not require an `import` statement to access anything defined in the same module. When you create a new project, your app is created inside a module with the same name as the Xcode target. If you have multiple targets in your project—for example, an app target and a test target—you simply import the module by specifying:

```
import TargetName
```

Swift

MAIN IS MISSING

The Xcode default templates are not just missing a few header files, they are also missing `main.m`. In the world of Objective-C, `main.m` contains the `main()` function that serves as the entry point for all C-based applications. Since you're now living in the world of Swift, you no longer need to implement `main()`, but you do need to carry out the same actions it would traditionally carry out.

Creating an equivalent `main.swift` is possible, but a new Swift feature can save writing this boilerplate code for many projects. Back in the sample project in Figure 1.2, the `AppDelegate.swift` file contains the following line above the declaration of the `AppDelegate` class:

```
@UIApplicationMain
```

Swift

This attribute is a hint to the Swift compiler that the subsequent class is suitable for use as an application delegate. Unfortunately, such convenience is not available if you need to create a custom subclass of UIApplication; in that case you'll need to resort to the old pattern of calling UIApplicationMain yourself. OS X projects have a similar attribute named @NSApplicationMain, which is also placed above a subclass of NSApplicationDelegate.

Swift introduces a number of these attributes that can be applied to declarations and types. Two of the most notable attributes, @IBAction and @IBOutlet, replace the corresponding definitions in Objective-C code for exposing outlet properties and action methods to Interface Builder. Later chapters examine the remaining attributes in more detail.

SEMICOLONS?

If you look through any of the template code in the Swift files generated by Xcode, you might notice that statements do not end with semicolons. This isn't a flaw in the templates; semicolons at the end of the line are now optional. Before you start reassigning that key to some other character, or attempt to pry it off your keyboard, bear in mind that they are no longer required but still have a number of purposes in Swift:

- Traditional for loops still use them.
- If you want to put two or more statements on one line (some people do), you need to separate them with a semicolon.
- If you work with a bunch of deviants who have a fetish for semicolons, they might still mandate that you use them. Get a new job.

USING SWIFT AND OBJECTIVE-C TOGETHER

Getting into Swift might seem like a big undertaking given the range of changes you've seen so far. Even the most experienced developers would be forgiven for being a bit reticent about getting stuck in a full-blown Swift project with a looming deadline right now.

Fortunately, it's not an all-or-nothing proposition. Apple has recognized that mixing and matching Swift with Objective-C is something developers are going to need for the foreseeable future, and even Apple has not yet ported its frameworks to Swift. Without the ability to use Swift and Objective-C in the same project, writing iOS and OS X apps in Swift right now would be impossible.

For more information about integrating Swift into Objective-C projects or re-using your Objective-C code in a new Swift project, see Chapter 15.

WRAPPING UP

At this stage, you should be able to create yourself a new Swift project and understand some of the fundamental differences between it and Objective-C. In the next chapter, you'll learn how to quickly dive into Swift without having to make that File > New > Project commitment that can often feel like a barrier to experimentation.

CHAPTER 2

Playgrounds and the Swift REPL

In software development, one of the biggest barriers to is getting past the initial hurdles.

For newcomers, learning Objective-C or Swift can be a challenge. The bewildering array of template options available when creating a new project or workspace can be off-putting.

Even for seasoned iOS or OS X developers, trying a new idea can be a frustrating experience. You have to choose a project type (and the hardest bit—give it a name), and use the same old build-and-run merry-go-round just to execute your code. And if your idea does seem like a good one, did you pick the right template up front, or do you need to go back, pick a new project, and copy the code over to it?

With Swift, Apple has introduced two new tools that make getting started an easier proposition. One is a REPL—an old standard, especially for scripting languages—which allows interactive programming using an environment known as a Read-Eval-Print-Loop. The other is Swift playgrounds, a unique development environment that is particularly useful for learning and experimentation with a minimum of hassle.

SWIFT PLAYGROUNDS

FIGURE 2.1 Playground creation options

FIGURE 2.2 An empty playground

Apple has striven to make creating a new Swift playground as straightforward as possible. The first option on the Welcome to Xcode screen is "Get started with a playground," or you can choose File > New > Playground from Xcode's main menu (shortcut: Command-Option-Shift-N). The dialog that appears allows you to name the playground and select whether your platform is iOS or OS X (**Figure 2.1**). In an ideal world, you wouldn't have to make any decisions before coding, but this is a substantial improvement on creating a full Xcode project or workspace.

After you set the name and platform options (you can choose iOS as your platform if you want to follow along), clicking Next prompts you to choose a location to save your playground file. Clicking Create opens the playground editor with a few sample lines of code to greet you. Welcome to your new playground!

A QUICK TOUR OF SWIFT PLAYGROUNDS

A playground is like most other Xcode editor windows but with a custom view of the world (**Figure 2.2**). The usual features like the toolbar, the navigator area, the debug area, and the utility area are all conspicuously absent. The reason is simple: You don't need them when working in a playground because your primary work environment is the source editor.

The source editor is almost identical to that which you normally use in a full Xcode project, but with one significant difference: a tinted sidebar to the right of the editor area. This sidebar is what makes a playground such an interactive environment for developing code and ideas.

```
4
5  var str = "Hello, Swift        ❶ Unterminated string literal  "Hello, Swift"
6
```

FIGURE 2.3 Xcode indicates a syntax error.

THE RESULTS SIDEBAR

A fresh iOS playground contains only two lines of code: The first is an import statement to make UIKit available, and the second defines a string variable. (Don't worry about the code or its syntax right now—we'll get to the differences between Swift and Objective-C in the next section.) The string variable contains the phrase Hello, playground—a variation on the classic "Hello, World!"

Interestingly, the Results sidebar also contains the phrase "Hello, playground" as though some magic inserts a hidden logging statement, compiles, and executes the code. It's actually not magic—just playgrounds in action.

As you insert, remove, or update code in the source editor, Xcode continually compiles the changes and executes the code for you, helpfully outputting the values of key variables along the way. Remember how you used to debug troublesome code caveman style by placing NSLog statements every time you made a modification to the variables? Now Xcode is doing it for you!

See for yourself by updating the string definition as follows:

```
var str = "Hello, Swift"
```
Swift

The Results sidebar updates as it detects changes in source code and changes to "Hello, Swift."

Now try something silly like removing the closing quotation mark from the end of the line. Xcode thinks about this change and then warns you with a red exclamation mark in the gutter of the source editor. Clicking the exclamation mark expands the error notification to give you a hint as to what you did wrong (**Figure 2.3**). The previous result in the sidebar is also dimmed to indicate a problem.

Putting the closing quotation mark back restores things to how they were before. Note that Xcode can also offer fix-it options in Swift playgrounds when it detects commonly encountered errors.

Although Xcode continually refreshes the Results sidebar in response to code changes (reminiscent of NSLog-debugging), it really comes into its own when you need to go back and modify existing statements. As an example, replace the string assignment statement with the following code:

```
var name = "Objective-C"
```
Swift

```
var str = "Hello, " + name
```

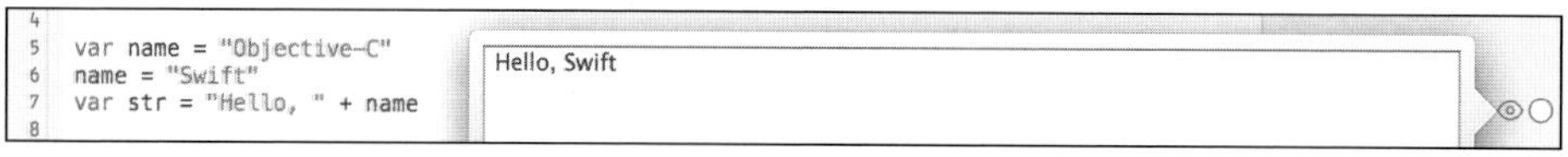

FIGURE 2.4 The Quick
Look popover

```
4
5   var name = "Objective-C"
6   name = "Swift"          Hello, Swift
7   var str = "Hello, " + name
8
```

FIGURE 2.4 The Quick
Look popover

The Results sidebar shows the values for the variables name and str at each stage with the resulting concatenation operation producing "Hello, Objective-C." Given that this is not correct, you might want to update name by inserting a corrective statement between the two:

Swift

```
var name = "Objective-C"
name = "Swift"
var str = "Hello, " + name
```

The Results sidebar updates to show the redefinition of name, and the output of the concatenation operation updates to reflect that one of its inputs has been changed. The power of this should be evident: You can develop complex logic in a visual way without time-consuming build and run cycles, or you can debug existing code without having to step linearly through lines of code in the debugger.

QUICK LOOK

You've only just started to delve into the power of playgrounds. Seeing the value of variables in the Results sidebar is great, but it would be nice to see more than just text. Moving your mouse pointer over a line in the sidebar highlights the line, and an eye-shaped Quick Look button appears. Mousing over the last line of the previous example and clicking the Quick Look button presents a popover (**Figure 2.4**) showing the text in more detail—handy if you are viewing long strings that might normally get truncated in the sidebar.

Straight text gets boring very quickly, so the Quick Look feature keeps your interest by displaying numerous data types, including the contents of collections, static images, and even UI elements. Try entering the following code to create a UIView and manipulate its content:

Swift

```
let parentView = UIView(frame: CGRectMake(0, 0, 200, 100))
parentView.backgroundColor = UIColor.redColor()

let childView = UIView(frame: CGRectMake(0, 0, 160, 60))
childView.backgroundColor = UIColor.whiteColor()

parentView.addSubview(childView)
childView.center = parentView.center

let label = UILabel(frame: CGRectMake(0, 0, 160, 60))
label.textAlignment = NSTextAlignment.Center
label.text = "Swift!"

childView.addSubview(label)
parentView
```

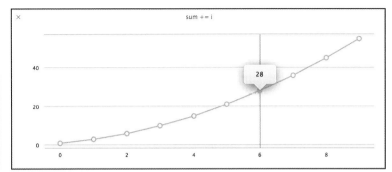

FIGURE 2.5 Quick Look preview of a UIView created in code

FIGURE 2.6 Timeline view for the expression `sum += i`

Clicking the Quick Look button on the line corresponding to the `parentView` statement produces a view like that shown in **Figure 2.5**. This could allow the design of custom UI elements without having to waste precious time running test applications in a simulator.

THE TIMELINE

Clicking the Quick Look button allows you to see a snapshot of the variable's value, but what if you want to see how the variable changes over time? Once again, Xcode has you covered with the Timeline feature of playgrounds. Enter the following code into the source editor:

```swift
var sum = 0
for (var i = 1; i <= 10; i++) {
   sum += i
}
```

Swift

The Results sidebar indicates that the line containing `sum += i` is executed 10 times and as a result is unable to display a simple value for it. Moving your mouse pointer over the sidebar reveals the Quick Look button and a circular Value History button to the right. Clicking the timeline icon causes the Assistant Editor to appear with a timeline view for the selected expression (**Figure 2.6**).

The timeline view contains a graph of the expression results plotted against time. Clicking a data point causes a popover to appear, showing its value at that point. At the bottom of the Assistant Editor is a scrubber control (like that in an audio player) and to its right a view with step controls to increment and decrement the time period.

You can use the scrubber to move backward and forward in time to see how a value changes in the timeline view, or if your view contains an animation you can use the step controls to determine how much should be shown.

Also available in the Assistant Editor is a console output view; any text written to the console by your code, the frameworks, or by third-party libraries causes the console output view to be displayed here.

WHAT CAN YOU DO WITH PLAYGROUNDS?

Playgrounds are a full development environment in which you can manipulate what is effectively a single Swift source file. You can create and use functions, classes, and other structures, and you have full access to the iOS and OS X frameworks so you can interact with way more than just your own code.

This makes playgrounds the ultimate scratch-pad for app development. Playgrounds can kick-start app ideas with a minimum of fuss, or can even be embedded within an existing project to let you try out new techniques without polluting existing code with your experiments.

One of the foremost examples that Apple demonstrated in the Swift announcement involved using SceneKit—an iOS and OS X animation framework that can be used in the production of games and other graphically intensive applications. Amazingly, you can use SceneKit directly in a playground, and you can develop SceneKit code that actually animates in the Quick Look popovers, and in the Assistant Editor, with advanced features such as collision detection working as you would expect from a live app. The Apple WWDC demo (named Balloons) is available as a downloadable playground from the Apple developer site: https://developer.apple.com/swift/blog/downloads/Balloons.zip.

A playground is also a great new way to debug code you are developing, or even older code in which you encountered a problem. With the traditional Xcode debugger, you are limited to a linear pathway through your code. With Swift, you can quickly adjust a value passed into a method or function and watch as the Results sidebar updates to show you how the change affects not just the output but also the intermediate steps. Alternatively, by calling a function in a loop, you can use a timeline to view how the output of the function changes across a range of values in a graphical plot.

There are limitations. From a security perspective, you are unable to make full use of system calls and although you can develop new UI controls and fine-tune their layouts in code, you cannot interact with them fully—buttons cannot be clicked, scrollviews cannot be scrolled, and text fields cannot accept input.

CREATING YOUR OWN PLAYGROUNDS

One of the potential future uses for Swift is that of education. The ease with which newcomers can open a playground and start typing Swift code significantly lowers the barriers to entry to Swift and to programming in general.

Apple has already demonstrated some of the potential through interactive documentation. The documentation for many Swift APIs now contains embedded playgrounds, which allow the reader to interact with the documentation in a way that has rarely been used to such great effect, which would make for an amazing teaching environment: A computer studies teacher could provide playgrounds containing lesson material with snippets of code embedded so that students could interact directly with it. So far Apple has provided no direct way for third parties to produce such material, but as usual the community has stepped up to the plate and come up with its own ways of doing so.

If you are familiar with NodeJS, you can install a third-party Node module that provides a command-line tool; when fed a Markdown document containing embedded Swift code blocks, the tool can produce a playground file that contains neatly formatted text interspersed with modifiable blocks of code. To find out more, have a look at the project home page at https://github.com/jas/swift-playground-builder.

THE SWIFT REPL

The Swift REPL is another type of interactive computing environment, but a slightly less visual variety. The basic premise is a command-line application that *reads* input from the user, *evaluates* the inputs, *prints* the output, and *loops* back again to accept more input.

You may be familiar with REPL environments if you have used languages such as Python or Ruby, in which the command line itself is a REPL for your shell of choice. When you type a simple shell command such as date, the shell reads your input, evaluates it, prints the date, and loops back to the shell prompt for your next command. The LLDB console debugger in Xcode is another REPL. They're everywhere! They're replicating!

HOW TO USE THE REPL

To use the Swift REPL you use the OS X Terminal application. At a shell prompt, type `xcrun swift`, and press Return to execute the command. You'll be prompted with the following:

```
Welcome to Swift!  Type :help for assistance.
  1>
```

If you don't get the REPL prompt, you may not be using the correct version of Xcode within the terminal. You can check your current Xcode version by typing `xcode-select -p` at the command line, which outputs the path that xcrun is currently using to find executables in the Xcode application bundle. If it is pointing to an Xcode version that does not support Swift, change it to an appropriate version (Xcode 6.1 and later) and try again:

```
sudo xcode-select -s /Applications/Xcode.app/Contents/Developer
```

To enter code into the REPL, just type at the prompt; the prompt is the number followed by a greater-than symbol (1>). When you press Return, it evaluates the input and decides what to do next. To follow tradition, enter the following highlighted code and press Return:

```
  1> println("Hello, World!")
```

"Hello, World!" prints to the screen, and the prompt number increments. The REPL prompt functions like many shell prompts and supports the use of the arrow keys for navigation. Press the Up and Down Arrow keys to navigate through your input history, and use the Left and Right Arrow keys to edit a line.

Single-line input is useful, but if you wanted to enter a control structure, having to type multiple statements on one line would be a hassle. Fortunately the REPL is smart enough to detect a multiline statement when you are entering it, and does not submit the individual statements for evaluation until it is completed; pressing Return takes you to a new line to enter the remaining statements. Note that a period (.) replaces the greater-than symbol (>) in the prompt to indicate that you are in the midst of a multiline statement. Try entering the following (syntactically incorrect) for loop:

```
2> for (i = 0; i < 3; i++) {
3. println("Hello, World!")
4. }
```

When you press Return after the last line, the REPL evaluates all the statements and prints its response. In this case, due to some poor Swift syntax, it prints an error message such as the following:

```
/var/folders/l8/0qgx4f7j343_t13ggc_5wk_r0000gn/T//lldb/60825/expr
→.GrmC27.swift:2:6: error: use of unresolved identifier 'i'
for (i = 0; i < 3; i++) {
     ^
```

Even though the start of the output looks like gibberish (it's actually the underlying location where the REPL is executing your code) the end shows that you used an unresolved identifier named i. It also helpfully shows at which point in the code the error occurs.

In Swift, you need to declare variables with the keyword var, so you need to go back and edit the first line of the multiline input. Pressing the Up Arrow once redisplays the complete three-line block, which you can then edit. Change the first line to read for (var i = 0; i < 3; i++) {. To resubmit, navigate to the end of the last line, and press Return again. This time you get three consecutive "Hello, World!" lines as you'd expect.

NOTE: Although the REPL editing facilities are quite advanced, they can still be tricky to work with so exercise caution. If you make a complex set of changes then accidentally press the Up Arrow key, you can lose those changes because the current code is replaced with the previous entry in the history.

If you have an issue with the code you've entered on a line, you can press Ctrl-C to discard the line. When you're finished working in the REPL, the quickest way to quit is to press Ctrl-D while the cursor is on an empty line.

POSSIBILITIES

So far, we've only looked at simple one-shot statements (albeit on single and multiple lines), which isn't particularly exciting beyond the initial learning period. We've also seen that the REPL can remember the commands you've previously entered, but that's not all it can remember. You can define a variable in one statement, and then reference it and even modify it later in another, as illustrated in the following session log:

```
  1> var i = 1
i: Int = 1
  2> ++i
$R0: Int = 2
  3> println(i)
2
```

When performing the variable creation and assignment, REPL outputs the type and value. On the next line, the result of pre-incrementing the variable is shown, and on the third line, the variable is used to print the current value of i to the console.

The REPL can accept all valid Swift code, so defining and using functions, classes, and structs is also possible. If your code is particularly long and complex, it may grow a bit frustrating to edit, but for shorter samples or experiments, the REPL proves an even quicker way to get writing code than playgrounds.

Given that you can use Swift to write pseudo-scripting language, the REPL is a great place to try potential script code. If you want to interact with the system, you can import modules such as Foundation, Cocoa, and AppKit, but if you go much further, you should create a playground or a full project.

So far we've only talked about using the REPL from the command line, but, because it is actually part of LLDB, it is also available from inside Xcode itself. To use it, just place a breakpoint in a full Swift project, and type `repl` at the LLDB prompt when the breakpoint has been reached; this allows you to execute code in the same environment that your application runs.

LIMITATIONS

The command line is not always the best environment in which to develop code (no matter what those Vim zealots try to tell you). The Swift REPL editing facilities are advanced compared to many similar environments, but it still doesn't have the text manipulation capabilities of a full-fledged editor like Xcode.

Compared to playgrounds the REPL is a much more linear environment. Although you can go back and edit statements you previously executed, the changes don't ripple through to the other objects and variables you have created since then. In a playground, you can change a value and watch the updates take place.

WRAPPING UP

Apple has taken enormous strides to make writing code easier, no matter what your reason for doing so. The hassles and pressures of creating an experimental development environment have been greatly reduced, allowing you to focus on creativity and not housekeeping.

In the next section of the book, we'll look at the actual syntax of the Swift language, with a particular focus on how it differs from Objective-C.

CHAPTER 3

Language Basics

Every programming book starts with the basics of the language for a reason: Without a grasp of the fundamental components, a firm understanding of the language is much harder to achieve. You could struggle through the concepts of higher-level constructs like classes and collections, but it becomes a real slog if you don't understand the building blocks like types, functions, and operators. Still, many experienced programmers skip over the first chapter or two, thinking they'll pick up the basics as they go along.

Swift and Objective-C are similar but not identical; they have some particularly crucial differences such as the basic types, functions, and variable/constant declarations. That's why the basics are even more important in this book and why we recommend that you open a playground and experiment with the concepts as you go along.

TYPES

The type system is fundamental to any programming language, and Swift is no different. For Objective-C users of course, there are some big differences. Swift was introduced as "Objective-C without the C," and much of the basic type system for Objective-C actually came from C. Swift therefore has its own basic types that are named and sometimes behave differently from what you might expect.

PRIMITIVE TYPES

C, Objective-C, and even C++ developers will be intimately familiar with C types. Stalwarts such as int, float, char, and friends have long been used to create more complex structs and classes; much of Apple's Foundation framework is written in C, and so the higher-level objects in Objective-C are built on these primitives. **Table 3.1** shows the Objective-C types side-by-side with their Swift counterparts:

NOTE: Table 3.1 assumes a 64-bit architecture for the sizing of the C primitive integer types. One nicety of Swift is that Int16 is always 16 bits regardless of the target platform.

USING PRIMITIVES AS OBJECTS

Swift types are all objects, which is a fundamental difference between the Objective-C primitives and the new Swift types. This will remind many Objective-C developers of using NSNumber in place of primitive types in collections, but the Swift types have a distinct advantage over NSNumber: They are mutable. This means you can create an Int variable named counter and increment using counter++.

It also allows Apple to extend the capabilities on primitive types, allowing for convenience methods like successor() and predecessor() on an integer type, as well as constructors that allow you to create an Int from other integer types. And of course, if Apple is able to extend the classes, so can you. Using extensions (the Swift equivalent to categories), you can truly make the primitive types your own.

USING TYPE ALIASES

If you are used to using C typedefs with your Objective-C code, Swift has you covered. If you want to apply a semantic meaning to a variable through its type, you can create a type alias using the typealias keyword. For example, if your code works with time intervals, you could create a type alias for Int named TimeInterval:

```
typealias TimeInterval = Int
```

You can now use TimeInterval when defining functions or data structures to express more meaning than you could with a generic integer type.

TABLE 3.1 Primitive Types

OBJECTIVE-C	SWIFT	NOTES
NSInteger	Int	Int is equivalent to Int32 on 32-bit machines, Int64 on 64-bit machines.
NSUInteger	UInt	UInt is equivalent to UInt32 on 32-bit machines, UInt64 on 64-bit machines.
char	Int8	If using char as an integer type, it is equivalent to Int8.
char	Character	If using as a character from a string, it is equivalent to a Character.
unsigned char	UInt8	
short	Int16	
unsigned short	UInt16	
int	Int32	
int	UInt32	
long	Int64	
unsigned long	UInt64	
long long	Int64	
unsigned long long	UInt64	
float	Float	
double	Double	
BOOL	Bool	Bool uses true and false—gone are the days of using YES and NO.
id	AnyObject	AnyObject is actually a protocol.
Class	None	There is no equivalent in Swift.
IMP	None	There is no equivalent in Swift.
SEL	Selector	This structure can return a textual representation of a selector.
void	Void	Void is equivalent to an empty tuple () and is rarely used directly.

STRINGS

Strings in the world of Objective-C come in two forms: native C strings and the Foundation-supplied `NSString`. These have long been the preferred options given the comparatively low-level nature of C strings; they are after all just null-terminated arrays of `char`s with a library of functions for manipulations.

Swift introduces its own native string type known simply as `String`. Its comprehensive set of functionality makes it comparable to `NSString` and has the ability to bridge with `NSString` objects. This allows you to use the `String` type in APIs where an `NSString` is expected.

But perhaps the nicest aspect of `String` objects is that they can be initialized without the @ sign we're so familiar with. We'll cover `String` in greater detail in Chapter 8.

FUNCTIONS

In Objective-C, a function had a very specific role that was distinct from a method; functions came from the world of C, were standalone, and didn't seem very object-oriented. In Swift the word "function" has a different meaning.

As in C, Swift supports the concept of standalone functions, and they are still very useful for creating one-off functions that don't rely on any state and thus do not need the baggage of creating an associated class.

In Objective-C we thought of methods as being separate from functions, but in Swift a method is simply a function that is "attached" to a class and can be called on an instance of that class. Swift functions can be used to attach methods to structures and enumerations, and can even be nested within other functions.

One primary difference between methods in Objective-C and functions in Swift is that in Swift a function is a type in itself; you can pass functions as parameters in function calls, and you can even return a function as the return value from a function call.

BLOCKS

The Swift equivalent to Objective-C's blocks are known as *closures*. This renaming of the concept brings us more in line with the rest of the programming world, but don't worry—your favorite foul-mouthed websites describing the syntax will no doubt be updated accordingly.

There are a number of differences between closures and blocks, primarily around the syntax. Closures have been subjected to a number of syntactical optimizations, such as trailing closure syntax and shorthand argument names, that in many simple cases make them much easier to read and understand.

TUPLES

Tuples are a completely new facet of Swift with no immediate parallel in Objective-C. In the world of mathematics, a tuple is a simple set of ordered data. The number of items in the set defines the type of tuple it is: 2 items form a 2-tuple, 3 items form a 3-tuple, and *n* items form an *n*-tuple.

You can define Swift tuples on-the-fly or as variables. When they're defined, you can name the individual items within the tuple or simply reference them by their index within the set. In many ways, they are like an extremely lightweight structure but with slightly less formality.

They also provide what has often been clamored for by Objective-C programmers. Tuples can be passed as parameters to functions and can be returned by functions; this effectively allows the use of multiple return values, something never-before possible without using structs or relying on the function modifying a parameter passed to it (known as an *out-parameter*).

CLASSES, STRUCTS, AND ENUMERATIONS

As you might expect from a modern object-oriented programming (OOP) language, Swift naturally supports the concept of classes. Many of the concepts remain the same with some syntactical changes, but there are some more significant differences:

- Swift classes do not need to inherit from a base class.
- All Swift instance variables are properties (there are no ivars).
- Swift classes follow a stricter form of access control.

Swift classes still support the concept of categories from Objective-C, but these are now known as *extensions*; this could be somewhat confusing if you originally came from a language such as Java that uses the extends keyword for inheritance.

The concept of a structure in Objective-C came straight from its C heritage; structures were particularly low level and best suited to simple data storage. Swift, however, takes the concept of a C structure and promotes it to a level similar to that of a class. Structures can now have methods, can mutate their own data, and even be enhanced with extensions.

The primary difference between a class and a structure is how they are passed—by reference or by value—and how they handle inheritance—classes do, structures do not. Structures in Objective-C were often shunned for their simplicity, but "should this really be a struct" is a question you should ask every time you type the word class in a Swift project.

To make matters even more confusing, Swift introduces an all-singing, all-dancing enumeration type that puts the lowly C enum to shame. Swift enumerations can not only handle integers, but they can also handle more complex data types, have associated data, and can have methods that act on the data.

Unlike Objective-C, Swift allows the nesting of complex object types inside other object types. This allows the embedding of an enumeration in a class, or a structure in a class, or a class in a structure (or any other combination you care to think of), bringing a greater level of encapsulation to Swift.

Your decision as to whether or not to use a class, structure, or enumeration to represent your data got a little bit harder with Swift.

COLLECTIONS

C has only one native collection type: arrays. C arrays are particularly basic when you are used to the power and convenience of NSArray and NSMutableArray, though these are actually provided by Foundation as opposed to Objective-C itself. Still, when we think of Objective-C we think of NSArray, NSDictionary, NSSet, and their mutable compatriots, as well as some of the more "obscure" collections like NSHashTable and NSMapTable.

Swift brings to the table its own native collections in the form of arrays and dictionaries. Unfortunately, it has no native equivalent to NSSet, but the good news is that the Foundation collections are all still available and can be used with your Swift code. In fact, in some cases when you're dealing with Objective-C APIs, you will have to use the Foundation collections.

Swift arrays and dictionaries are comparable to their Objective-C equivalents in both functionality and performance, and using them wherever possible makes sense. They also go further in many respects, adding modern functionality (like map, filter, and reduce functions to arrays).

VARIABLE DECLARATIONS

One of the starkest differences between Swift and Objective-C is in how you declare a variable. Creating and assigning values to variables is a fundamental part of any language, and getting used to some of the changes Swift brings can take a while.

VAR AND LET

Objective-C followed the old C pattern using:

Objective-C

```
type name = assignment;
```

So if you wanted to create an integer variable named counter with an initial value of 0, you would use:

Objective-C

```
NSInteger counter = 0;
```

Swift, on the other hand, uses the following format:

Swift

```
var name: type = assignment
```

And so the equivalent declaration for counter would be:

Swift

```
var counter: Int = 0
```

So why the var keyword? It seems a bit on the redundant side, and a little too much like JavaScript for comfort. Relax though, it has a purpose, and that purpose is to distinguish between variables and constants. To declare a constant in Swift, you use the following form:

Swift

```
let name: type = assignment
```

So to create a constant defining a maximum value for the counter, you would do so as follows:

```swift
let maxCounter: Int = 10
```
Swift

As with Objective-C, creating a variable in advance of assigning it is perfectly valid, although you must not use the variable until it has been initialized.

```swift
var deferredCounter: Int
```
Swift

```swift
// Other code can go here, as long as it does not
// reference the deferredCounter variable

deferredCounter = 0
```

This is not the case with constants—they must be initialized at the time of declaration. Note that the only thing that is actually constant about a constant is the reference to the data. If your constant points to an instance of a class or a struct, you cannot change the constant to point to another instance. You can however modify the data within that instance:

```swift
class IntContainer { var internalInt: Int = 0 }
let intContainer = IntContainer()
intContainer.internalInt = 3
```
Swift

MUTABILITY

You may be wondering why there is a dedicated syntax for creating constants—after all, in a lot of Objective-C code, constants are not used nearly as often as variables. This may be a result of culture, or because constants don't always feel like a part of the Objective-C language. Where constants are used, they are often just declared using C-preprocessors macros (#define statements), and are less often declared using the const keyword (again a feature of C rather than Objective-C). Defining a constant elsewhere, or adding an extra keyword to a variable declaration, can lead a lazy or impatient developer to just settle for regular variables instead of constants.

Swift on the other hand attempts to promote safety within your code. You can make a choice between var and let at the point of declaration, and you don't need an extra keyword; the alternatives are the same length in characters, which is probably coincidental but a happy coincidence nonetheless.

The concept of using constants may seem a bit strange to Objective-C developers, but in many respects we've been doing so for many years. When you create an NSString instead of an NSMutableString, or an NSArray instead of an NSMutableArray, you've elected to use a constant instead of a variable; in the Foundation framework we just use the terminology *mutable* and *immutable*.

FIGURE 3.1 Xcode can display the inferred type.

Making a type mutable or immutable by changing a single keyword is a huge step forward toward safer code. Following a practice of using immutables (constants) until you find a need to change their value can also lead to your code being more easily optimizable by the compiler, and faster to execute. Not having to change class types (for example between `NSString` and `NSMutableString`) makes switching between mutable and immutable variants simpler when the time arises.

TYPE INFERENCE

A frequent complaint about strongly typed languages like C and Objective-C is that developers must think about their variables' types when they declare them. The advantage to this is *type safety*—when you define a variable as a specific type you can't assign a different type to it without a compiler or runtime error.

In languages where type safety is not enforced, developers can reassign many different types to a variable over the course of its life. This is great from a flexibility point of view, but can lead to unexpected results if not used with care.

Swift attempts to find a middle ground between the rigidity of type safety and the flexibility of not having to explicitly define your types. It achieves this through the technique known as *type inference*.

So far in this book, we've been explicit in most of the declarations—we didn't want to spoil the type inference surprise—and have been using the following form for declarations:

Swift
```
var name: type = assignment
```

When the type can be inferred from the assignment, you can instead use the shortened form:

Swift
```
var name = assignment
```

To use type inference, you need to assign a value to your variable immediately; otherwise the type cannot be inferred. You don't have to assign a literal value—it could be an assignment from an expression or the return value from a function.

Swift
```
var inferredCounter = UInt.min
```

In this example, `UInt.min` is a function that returns the minimum valid value for a `UInt`, which is zero. The type of the `min` property is a `UInt` so that is the type assumed for `inferredCounter`.

While type inference is a great way to speed up the process of writing—and even reading—code, try to exercise care when you do so. If you are assigning a function return value, ensure that the function name is expressive and is reasonably clear about what type is being returned. If you are inspecting code and are having trouble telling what type is being inferred, Option-clicking the variable name displays a popover showing the inferred type (**Figure 3.1**).

SYNTAX

A number of basic syntactical changes to Swift may cause confusion for Objective-C developers. We have tried to detail the most important here, but we cover countless other minor changes in other sections as we stumble across them.

SEMICOLONS

Possibly the most striking change is that the semicolon is no longer required at the end of statements. You can still use semicolons if you prefer, but terminating your statements with a semicolon is optional.

At this stage no one knows whether the use of semicolons to terminate statements will decline as Swift is adopted. Unfortunately, by making it optional Apple has introduced another way to create style-guide conflicts within development teams and open-source projects, so the best advice we can give is to choose what suits you, and then be prepared to adopt the practices of the team you work with. The examples in this book do not use semicolons—make of that what you will.

Semicolons are still required by the compiler in two places:

- When placing multiple statements on a single line, the statements must be separated using semicolons. However, putting multiple statements on a single line is not a common use case and hinders readability when debugging code, so we recommend not doing it.
- When using a traditional for loop, you must use a semicolon to separate the initializer, conditional, and loop expressions.

WHERE IS @?

One of the signature aspects of Objective-C syntax has been the increasing use of the at sign (@) in recent years. The character has long been used in the declaration of classes, properties, and string literals, but its use increased dramatically as new literal syntax for Booleans, numbers, arrays, and dictionaries was introduced a few years ago.

Swift eschews the @ in many of the places where Objective-C currently uses it. **Table 3.2** shows a comparison of the respective use cases in Objective-C and Swift.

Swift still uses the @ in many places, but as a way of adding attributes to other keywords; when indicating that a class should be used as the main entry point to an application, the attribute @UIApplicationMain is used. Usages of @ in Swift will be noted as we progress through the book.

TABLE 3.2 Where the @ Is Missing

USE CASE	OBJECTIVE-C SYNTAX	SWIFT EQUIVALENT
Declaring a string literal	`@"Hello, World!"`	`"Hello, World!"`
Declaring a number literal	`@1.23`	`1.23`
Declaring a Boolean literal	`@YES`	`true`
Declaring an array literal	`@[ var1, var2 ]`	`[ var1, var2 ]`
Declaring a dictionary literal	`@{ var1: var2 }`	`[ var1: var2 ]`
String literal variable substitution	`@"%@", variable`	`"\(variable)"`

Declaring class interface and implementation	`@interface MyClass`
	`@end`
	`@implementation MyClass`
	`@end`
		`class MyClass {`
		`}`

Declaring a class property	`@property () propname`	`var propname`

NO LONGER HIP TO BE SQUARE

When first confronted with Objective-C, a developer's eyes are often immediately drawn to the extensive use of square brackets throughout the code. For a long time, the only way to send a message to an object (the Objective-C equivalent of calling a method) was through the use of square brackets. More recently, Apple introduced dot-syntax, which allowed a user to access properties using the dot operator, which made the language a bit more like Java or C++.

Unfortunately for those who dislike dot-syntax, Apple has decided it will be the way to invoke methods on classes, structures, and enumerations in Swift. For more information about how to invoke a method, see the section "Functions" earlier in this chapter.

Fans of the square bracket should not worry—it will not be completely retired and will still be used for declaring array literals, and will even be replacing the curly brace for declaring dictionary literals.

CONTROL BLOCKS

Control blocks, such as `if`, `for`, `while`, and `switch` are all subject to changes that will affect all Objective-C developers. The general format remains the same, but a huge change is that the curly brackets are no longer optional.

Some have speculated that this was inspired by the infamous "goto bug"—where a decision to not use curly brackets resulted in a huge security vulnerability and potential embarrassment for Apple—but we'll probably never know for sure. It is true though that in Swift the same problem could not occur because curly brackets are required.

Going in the other direction, the designers of Swift have decided that the parentheses, which were previously mandatory, can now be omitted. The following are all now valid constructs in Swift:

- `if condition { ... }.`
- `for initialization; condition; loop { ... }.`
- `while condition { ... }.`
- `switch variable { ... }.`

As with semicolons, the omission of parentheses will likely be determined by the preferences of whoever creates your style guide. Our preference is to omit them, so we ignore them from here on.

THE POST-PREPROCESSOR AGE

If you ever used statements that began with a hash mark in Objective-C, you were actually taking advantage of the C preprocessor. This includes statements such as `#define`, `#ifdef`, and `#pragma`, as well as macro substitution for variables you have defined or are defined by the preprocessor (such as `__FILE__`, `__LINE__`, and so on).

Adhering to its tagline of being "Objective-C without the C," Swift also does away with the C preprocessor, which means that you can no longer take advantage of the full range of preprocessor directives.

One of the primary uses for preprocessor directives is in the conditional compilation of code, for example in a debug build. The Swift developers have included a basic alternative that supports the `#if`, `#elseif`, `#else`, and `#endif` keywords. The `#if` and `#elseif` statements support testing build configurations (such as operating system/architecture) and command-line flags.

Many Objective-C developers also take advantage of the `#pragma mark` directive to insert markers in the document structure view (**Figure 3.2**) in Xcode. You can achieve the same behavior in Swift using one of the specially formatted comments shown in the following list. Xcode also supports the ability to add `TODO` and `FIXME` comments (a particular favorite of developers) so that they can be seen directly in the document structure.

- `// MARK: comment` — includes a plain marker
- `// MARK: - comment` — includes a marker with a line preceding it
- `// TODO: comment`
- `// FIXME: comment`

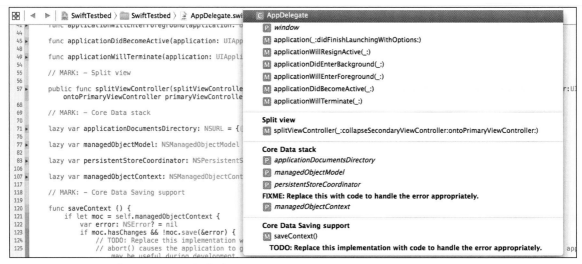

FIGURE 3.2 `MARK`, `TODO`, and `FIXME` comments in the document structure

FIGURE 3.3 Viewing documentation comments in Xcode

```
30   /**
31   A Basic Class
32
33   Performs some basic activities and leads a boring life
34
35   Additional paragraphs of information
36
37   :Sectio          Declaration    class func createBasicClassWithBasicProperty(#
38                                   basicProperty: String) -> BasicClass
39   Some mo
40   */               Description    Creates a BasicClass
41   class B
42       ///                         This is a bit more detail on the method
43       var                         createBasicClassWithBasicProperty. The parameters will be detailed
44                                   below using special keywords, as will the return value.
45       ///          Parameters     basicProperty    a String containing a basic property
46       ///
47       ///          Returns        a configured BasicClass
48       ///
49       ///          Declared In    CH3 - Language Basics.playground
50       /// :param: basicProperty a String containing a basic property
51       /// :returns: a configured BasicClass
52       class func createBasicClassWithBasicProperty(# basicProperty: String) -> BasicClass {
53           let basicClass: BasicClass = BasicClass()
54           basicClass.basicProperty = basicProperty
55           return basicClass
56       }
57   }
```

COMMENTS

While on the subject of comments, Swift uses the same comment styles as Objective-C with some additional features. Multiline (or block) comments can now be nested. No longer must a small multiline comment interfere with temporarily commenting out a larger section of code.

While it has yet to be fully documented by Apple, an additional comment style can be used to attach formatted documentation to your classes and methods. If you're familiar with the Javadoc or Doxygen formats, you might find this all familiar. The following code shows a class with a property and method documented using this syntax. **Figure 3.3** shows the output provided by Xcode when Option-clicking a documented identifier in your code.

```
/**
    A Basic Class

    Performs some basic activities and leads a boring life

    Additional paragraphs of information

    :Section Header:

    Some more information.
 */
class BasicClass {
    /// A String property containing Stringy information
    var basicProperty: String = ""

    /// Creates a BasicClass
    ///
    /// This is a bit more detail on the method
  ⇢ createBasicClassWithBasicProperty. The parameters
    /// will be detailed below using special keywords, as will the return value.
    ///
    /// :param: basicProperty a String containing a basic property
    /// :returns: a configured BasicClass
    class func createBasicClassWithBasicProperty(# basicProperty: String) ->
  ⇢ BasicClass {
        let basicClass: BasicClass = BasicClass()
        basicClass.basicProperty = basicProperty
        return basicClass
    }
}
```

OPERATORS

Swift's operators can be broken down into three main categories:

- Identical to their Objective-C counterparts
- Different from their Objective-C counterparts
- New to Swift with no direct equivalent in Objective-C

IDENTICAL

Thankfully, Apple has elected not to mess around with the basics, so many of the traditional operators you know and love have the same meanings and behaviors in Swift. **Table 3.3** shows the operators that have stayed true to themselves in these changing times:

TABLE 3.3 Unchanged Objective-C/Swift Operators

OPERATOR	BEHAVIOR	OPERATOR	BEHAVIOR
+	Addition	&=	Bitwise AND and assignment
-	Subtraction	|	Bitwise OR
*	Multiplication	|=	Bitwise OR and assignment
/	Division	^	Bitwise XOR
%	Remainder	^=	Bitwise XOR and assignment
=	Assignment	!	Logical NOT
+=	Addition and assignment	&&	Logical AND
-=	Subtraction and assignment	||	Logical OR
*=	Multiplication and assignment	<<	Bit shift left
/=	Division and assignment	>>	Bit shift right
<	Less-than comparison	<<=	Bit shift left and assignment
<=	Less-than or equal-to comparison	>>=	Bit shift right and assignment
>	Greater-than comparison	++	Increment (prefix and postfix)
>=	Greater-than or equal-to comparison	--	Decrement (prefix and postfix)
&	Bitwise AND		

DIFFERENT

Apple has changed how some of the existing Objective-C operators work. **Table 3.4** shows the operators that have different meanings in Swift.

EQUALITY OPERATOR CHANGES

A common mistake newcomers to Objective-C will make is in trying to use the equality operator to compare the values of objects—for example, comparing two distinct NSNumber objects that may have the same numerical value. Objective-C's equality operator will compare only the primitive types, and so comparing two objects will result in a very simple pointer comparison. The proper way to compare two objects is to use the -[NSObject isEqual:] method, which, if properly implemented by a class, will perform a real comparison between the data of two objects.

TABLE 3.4 Different Objective-C/Swift Operators

OPERATOR	BEHAVIOR
==	Equal
!=	Not equal
&+	Addition with overflow
&-	Subtraction with overflow
&*	Multiply and ignore overflow
&/	Divide and ignore overflow
&%	Remainder and ignore overflow
%=	Remainder and assignment
&&=	Logical AND and assignment
||=	Logical OR and assignment
.	Member access
?:	Ternary operator (*only* as a ternary operator, not in the shortcut version)

Swift's equality operator is different and behaves much as newcomers might expect, but not necessarily how Objective-C developers might expect. Through the magic of operator overloading (which we cover in detail in Chapter 14), you create your own definitions for how the equals (==) and not-equal (!=) operator should behave when applied to object types.

While this requires a little bit more forethought when creating object types, it can lead to much more readable code and is worth investing the extra time needed to create the required overloads.

OVERFLOW CHANGES

Swift has a collection of new operators you could be forgiven for thinking relate to AND operations given that they all start with an ampersand. In reality, they are all variations on the standard operators with respect to how they deal with overflow situations.

In the case of addition and subtraction, overflow is taken into account. For example if you were to try the following in Objective-C, you would end up with a compiler warning (which you may or may not be able to live with):

```
unsigned char withoutOverflow = 230 + 50;
```
Objective-C

If you were to try the same in Swift, you would be confronted with an error rather than a simple warning:

```
var withoutOverflow: UInt8 = 230 + 50
```
Swift

Swift offers the addition with overflow operator (&+), which allows the result to wrap around if you so desire it:

Swift

```
var withOverflow: UInt8 = 230 &+ 50
```

Note that this may appear to work with Objective-C as well, but the result is different:

Objective-C

```
unsigned char withOverflow = 230 &+ 50;
```

In fact, this expression is actually 230 & (+50) and so performs a bitwise AND operation on 230 using a value of 50. In Objective-C, the following expressions are all the same:

- 230&+50
- 230 &+50
- 230 & +50
- 230 & + 50
- 230& +50
- 230&+ 50

Swift is stricter, which is how 230 & +50 can be discerned from 230 &+ 50. If you're the sort of developer who likes to play fast and loose with whitespace, you may want to pay a little bit more attention to it in future.

ASSIGNMENT OPERATOR CHANGES

Developers often fall into two camps: those who believe that assignment operators are an unnecessary way to achieve terseness and lower readability in your code, and those who are wrong. If you fall into the latter camp you may be pleased to know that the Swift language introduces some extra assignment operators with which you can make your code illegible:

- Remainder and assignment (%=)
- Logical AND and assignment (&&=)
- Logical OR and assignment (||=)

Perfect for the inaugural Swift code obfuscation contest when it inevitably takes place.

> **NOTE:** Your author prefers a more verbose coding style, and to let the compiler do the optimization. Just in case it isn't obvious.

OTHERS

Once upon a time, the only way to set or get properties in Objective-C was by doing things the long way using the -propertyName and -setPropertyName: syntax. Some Objective-C developers looked on jealously while C++ and Java developers used a nice simple dot notation—even C structs had been in on the party. Eventually, Apple enhanced Objective-C to support *dot-syntax*, a shorthand way to call the accessor methods on a class. Depending on the side of the fence you came down on, this was either a great step forward or you were living in the past. Dot-syntax has been codified into Swift as the only way to access the functions or data from an instance by using the member access operator, also known as the humble period or full-stop.

Swift retains the ternary operator but does break with a recent change to its use in Objective-C. The GNU C compiler introduced a shorthand form that condensed the following syntax:

```
value ? value : altValue;
```

to this

```
value ?: altValue;
```

Swift demands that the ternary operator take three operands; so if you learned this shorthand, now may be the time to unlearn it.

NEW

Swift not only modifies the behavior of some existing operators, it also introduces some completely new operators. **Table 3.5** summarizes those that are new to Swift.

RANGE OPERATORS

The range operators are the *half-open range* (..<) and the *closed range* (...). Despite their confusing names and syntax (surely ... should be open and ..< should be half-closed?), they are still very useful operators, especially when working with for loops. The closed range can be used to produce a range of values that includes the left operand, and the integer steps between, up to, and including the right operand. The expression 3...6 produces a set of values containing 3, 4, 5, and 6. When used in a for-in loop, the range can be assigned to a variable to be used within the loop, similar to iterating over a collection in Objective-C. The following loop will print the current value of counter four times:

```
for counter in 3...6 {
    println(counter)
}
```

Swift

TABLE 3.5 NEW Swift Operators

OPERATOR	BEHAVIOR
~	Bitwise NOT
..<	Half-open range
...	Closed range
?	Optional chaining
!	Forced unwrap
??	Nil coalescing
is	Compare to type
as	Cast to type
as?	Cast to optional type
===	Identical
!==	Not identical
~=	Pattern matching
[]	Subscript
[]=	Subscript assignment

The half-open range operator behaves very much the same but does not include the last value of the range. The expression 3..<6 produces a set containing just three values: 3, 4, and 5. The following loop will print the current value of counter just three times:

Swift

```
for counter in 3..<6 {
    println(counter)
}
```

If you find yourself struggling to remember what values the different range operators produce, think of the less-than symbol in the half-open variant (..<) as indicating that it includes values less than the right operand.

OPTIONAL OPERATORS

The optional operators—optional chaining (?), forced unwrap (!), and nil coalescing (??)—have been added to support the optional types feature of Swift. Because optional types are a new concept to Objective-C developers, all of Chapter 5 is devoted to them, and explains how to use these new operators.

TYPE OPERATORS

The type operators could be seen as having equivalents in Objective-C, but given the difference in usage they could be considered completely new operators. Considering that they are based around English words, they seem even more new and unusual.

First is the is operator, which can be considered as the "type comparison" or "type check" operator. It is a binary expression operator, like && or ||, and attempts a type cast on the left-side expression to the type specified on the right side. If the left expression can be cast successfully, the operator returns true, otherwise it returns false. The left-side expression is not modified as part of the process.

This may seem familiar because it acts in a way similar to the Objective-C method -[NSObject isKindOfClass:]. The is operator goes one step further though, and also supports the comparison of an expression to a protocol. In this way, it also replaces the Objective-C method -[NSObject conformsToProtocol:].

A common pattern in Objective-C is to check if a reference is a type of class, and then cast the reference down to the class:

Objective-C

```
UIView *view = [UILabel new];
if ([view isKindOfClass:[UILabel class]]) {
    UILabel *label = (UILabel*)view;
}
```

Instead of using the Objective-C style of type cast—(UILabel *)—Swift introduces a new operator named as. The previous example could instead be written as:

Swift

```
let view: UIView = UILabel();
if view is UILabel {
    let label = view as UILabel
}
```

Note that you should use the typecast operator only when you know that the expression you are attempting to downcast is of the correct type. In the previous example, we checked it first using the is operator, but this can be an unwieldy pattern—constant if blocks grow tiresome to write and to read. Fortunately, there is an additional variant of the as operator you can use when working with optionals: as?. We'll take a look at optionals in greater detail in Chapter 5.

IDENTICAL/NOT-IDENTICAL

A side effect of the behavioral changes to the equals (==) and not equal (!=) operators is that comparing two object references to determine if they point to the same object is no longer possible. To overcome this limitation, Swift introduces the *identical* (===) and *not identical* (!==) operators. The identical operator will return true if the left and right expressions resolve to the same object, and false if they don't. The not identical operator does the opposite, as you would expect.

PATTERN MATCH OPERATOR

If you have used Perl, you may notice a similarity between Swift's pattern match operator ~= and Perl's "regular expression" operator =~. Although you might think that an operator that looks so similar (and is called the "pattern match" operator) must also work with regular expressions, you would be wrong. Sort of.

By default, the pattern match operator can match a number of pattern types, but regular expressions are not one of them. You can, however, use it to match tuples, ranges, and even wildcards.

For example, in Objective-C, if you wanted to determine if a value fell with a particular range, you would write a conditional like the following:

```
if (integerValue > 0 && integerValue < 10) {
    NSLog(@"integer value is in range 1 to 9");
}
```
Objective-C

With Swift's pattern match operator, you can now write:

```
if 1...9 ~= integerValue {
    println("integer value is in range 1 to 9")
}
```
Swift

You can extend Swift's pattern matching capabilities by overloading the ~= operator, and you can also use this functionality in while loops. The primary use case seems to be switch statements, although without the operator, so we'll look at using patterns in more detail in Chapter 4.

SUBSCRIPT OPERATORS

At the same time they introduced array and literal syntax to Objective-C, Apple also allowed developers to apply a similar syntax to their own data structures. This syntax is known as subscript notation and is also available in Swift. We cover how you enable this functionality in your own classes, structures, and enumerations in Chapter 10, but for now we'll settle for introducing the two subscript operators.

The first is simply known as the subscript operator ([ ]) and can be used to access a value for a given parameter, just like accessing an array value at a given index. The second operator is the subscript assignment operator ([ ]=) and is used to create or update a value for a given parameter, again like setting a value in an array for a given index.

TUPLES

In Swift a tuple is a lightweight data structure that contains a list of values. Unlike object types, tuples can have no functions associated with them, and in many ways they are closer to C structs than Swift's own structure type. Unlike C structs however, Swift tuples can be created and defined on demand as opposed to being specified somewhere as a formal type. Formally creating and reusing a tuple "type" is possible, but their quick and dirty nature means that many tuples will be defined as and when they are needed. Whether this is a good or bad thing remains to be seen.

You can put just about anything into a tuple (primitives, objects, other tuples), and you can make it as big as you like. But bear in mind that as the amount and complexity of the data grows, the harder it will be to use, and the more likely you'll be to benefit from using a more formal data structure.

CREATING AND USING TUPLES

To create, or compose, a tuple you simply assign it to a variable or constant:

Swift

```
let coordinate = (3, 2)
```

To retrieve the data from a tuple, you can reference the individual values using the member access operator (.) and specifying a number corresponding to the index of the value you want. In the previous example, coordinate contains two values so the indexes are 0 and 1. Thus you can access the first value using coordinate.0 and the second value using coordinate.1.

If you prefer accessing the data using more meaningful identifiers, you can name your values as they go into the tuple. To follow convention, you can redefine coordinate using x and y coordinates:

Swift

```
let coordinate = (x: 3, y: 2)
```

You can now access the data using coordinate.x and coordinate.y, which is much more intuitive.

As an alternative to diving into the structure of a tuple, you can instead use a technique known as *decomposing* to assign individual values from the tuple to variables you specify:

```Swift
let (x, y) = coordinate
```

Now the variables x and y will contain the first and second values from coordinate.

If you don't care what the value of x will be, Swift allows you a *wildcard* variable (_) that can be used instead of x. The value will be retrieved and then discarded:

```Swift
let (_, y) = coordinate
```

We'll look at wildcards in more detail in the "Switch" section of Chapter 4.

REUSING TUPLES

If you have a simple data structure you would like to model as a tuple, but would prefer it to have a type, there is a solution for you. Swift provides an equivalent to C's typedef known as typealias that can be used to give alternative names to types; this is particularly useful when you have tuples that have no name.

If you wanted to give a coordinate system an extra dimension, and name it at the same time, you could use the following code:

```Swift
typealias ThreeDCoordinate = (x: Int, y: Int, z: Int)
let originPoint: ThreeDCoordinate = (0, 0, 0)
```

You can also use the type alias as a type in function definitions, or for creating properties in more complex data structures.

WRAPPING UP

Don't worry if you found this chapter to be tough going. Becoming familiar with the basics of any language is essential if you want to understand the higher-level topics.

In the next chapter, you'll learn more about Swift's control structures that allow you to make decisions within your code.

CHAPTER 4

Control Structures

Working with data is difficult if you have to do it in a completely linear manner, which makes control structures a vital part of any programming language. On the surface, the control structures in Swift are the same as those in Objective-C, but once you start to dig a little deeper you will begin to find that they go beyond what was possible before in a number of ways.

GENERAL CHANGES

Like Objective-C, Swift has four main control structures:

- `for` and `for-in` loops
- `while` and `do-while` loops
- `if` conditional blocks
- `switch` conditional blocks

They behave in a similar manner to their Objective-C counterparts but with some key differences you should be aware of.

PARENTHESES ARE OPTIONAL

The parentheses that surround the conditionals of the `if`, `for`, and `while` structures are no longer mandatory. Similarly the parentheses that surround the `switch` expression are also no longer mandatory.

This for loop:

```
for (var i = 0; i < 3; i++) { ... }
```

can now be written with less punctuation as:

```
for var i = 0; i < 3; i++ { ... }
```

BRACES ARE MANDATORY

As if to provide a counterbalance, the Swift developers have made curly braces mandatory for control structure blocks that contain a single line of code. An `if` statement in Objective-C that takes advantage of this shortcut:

```
if (number < 0)
    NSLog(@"Negative number");
else if (number > 0)
    NSLog(@"Positive number");
else
    NSLog(@"Zero");
```

has to be fully fleshed out in Swift:

```
if number < 0 {
    println("Negative number")
} else if number > 0 {
    println("Positive number")
} else {
    println("Zero")
}
```

Enforcing the use of braces may be a source of annoyance to developers who like to keep single-line `if` statements compact, but should result in safer code for many others.

BOOLEAN CONDITIONS

The `if` conditional in C (and thus Objective-C) behaves in a manner summarized very simply: If the supplied expression evaluates to `true` then the `if` block is executed. Where things get complicated is in the number of ways an expression can evaluate to `true`. The following list shows the variety of positive evaluations:

- A Boolean expression that evaluates to `true`
- A Boolean expression that evaluates to `YES`
- A numerical value that is nonzero (positive or negative)
- An object pointer that is not `nil`
- A pointer that is not `NULL`

In Objective-C, this allows us to take some convenient shortcuts. For example, testing for nonzero numbers is a common pattern:

```
if (integerValue) {
    // Perform an action if not zero
}
```
Objective-C

Swift relies heavily on protocols to define behavior, and one such protocol is Boolean-Type. An expression can be used only as a conditional if it conforms to this protocol, and even the humble `Int` does not conform by default. To use a conditional, you just need to be more specific about what exactly it is you are testing:

```
if integerValue != 0 {
    // Perform an action if not zero
}
```
Swift

This may seem like a pain at first, but is actually a useful way to learn some good programming practices. When we relied on the fact that a nonzero number equated to `true`, we also assumed that the reader of the code knew our exact meaning. This is acceptable with precise numbers, but could easily get confusing when working with enums or any other types where an assumption is being made that the reader knows the underlying values. The Swift core principle of safety is the likely motive behind these changes; making conditionals more explicit means less likelihood of using them incorrectly and getting unexpected results.

Now that we've covered the general differences, let's look into the four control structures in detail.

LOOPS

As with Objective-C, Swift has two flavors of loops—for and while—each of which has its own two varieties. The `for` statement supports the traditional C-style `for` statement with initializer, conditional, and increment expressions, and the more modern `for-in` style that works with collections and other iterable constructs. The `while` statement supports condition-block execution, and the `do-while` supports block-condition execution.

FOR AND FOR-IN

The traditional for loop works exactly as you would expect. The general format is still for *initializer*; *conditional*; *increment* with the only differences being in how the initializer and conditional are expressed:

- You must define variables using the var keyword; you can't subsequently increment a constant.
- You can rely on type inference to set the correct type for newly defined variables.
- You must use a conditional that conforms to the BooleanType protocol.

The `for-in`-style of loop has seen more in the way of changes with Swift. `for-in` was introduced with *fast enumeration* in Objective-C and is available to any classes that implement the NSFastEnumeration protocol. Objective-C developers most frequently use `for-in` loops with NSArray, NSSet, and NSDictionary collections, though any NSEnumerator-based class will also conform to NSFastEnumeration.

In Swift, the counterpart to the NSFastEnumeration protocol is SequenceType, and so anything that conforms to SequenceType is iterable. As you would expect, the default collections (array and dictionary) do so, but a few other types also implement the protocol:

- Foundation collection types—Apple has performed the requisite magic to allow the collection types you know and love to behave as iterable collections in Swift.
- Strings—A string is, after all, a collection of characters, and so the Swift String type supports iterating over the characters in a string.
- Half-open and closed ranges—Both types of ranges appear to the `for-in` loop as a collection of integers allowing it to iterate over the items in the collection.
- strides—The Swift stride function can be used to produce more complex ranges, including configurable increments and descending ranges.

Being able to use ranges with a `for-in` loop means fewer reasons than ever before to use the traditional for loop. Where you once used the following to perform a block of actions 10 times:

Objective-C
```
for var i = 1; i <= 10; i++ { ... }
```

you can now use a range with the for-in variant instead:

```Swift
for i in 1...10 { ... }
```

Note how this improves readability; there is less chance of off-by-one errors, and if you're the type of developer who sweats the naming of your variables, you can even use a wildcard expression to show that you don't care what the variable is:

```Swift
for _ in 1...10 { ... }
```

If you want to make your own object types iterable, you need to implement the SequenceType protocol. We will look at protocols in more detail in Chapter 13.

WHILE AND DO-WHILE

There is not much difference between while and do-while loops in Objective-C and Swift. Aside from the general changes described earlier (regarding conditions, parentheses, and braces), the only other difference you are likely to encounter is in the use of optional binding, which can be used as an alternative to using a != nil test in a conditional expression.

For example, say you wanted to travel up a UIView hierarchy to determine the topmost view—indicated by the superview property being nil. In Objective-C, you would do the following:

```Objective-C
UIView *currentView = aView;

while (currentView.superview != nil) {
    currentView = currentView.superview;
}
```

Using optional binding in Swift, you can instead use this code:

```Swift
var possibleView: UIView? = aView
while let actualView = possibleView?.superview {
    possibleView = actualView
}
```

Don't worry if the excessive question marks seem a bit strange—we introduce optionals and optional binding in Chapter 5.

CONDITIONALS

Conditionals in Swift also come in the same two types as Objective-C: the largely unchanged if statement and the radically overhauled switch statement.

IF

Like while loops, the if conditional statement in Swift has mainly the same behaviors as its counterpart in Objective-C. As with the other control statements, it is subject to the changes in parentheses and braces, and again requires the conditional expression to conform to the BooleanType. Also like the while statement, if can be used with optional binding to guard against optional variables whose current value is nil.

SWITCH

Of all the flow control statements, the humble switch has probably changed the most. In Objective-C, describing switch as an alternative way of writing a series of if statements would be fair. For example, consider this sequence of if statements:

Objective-C

```
if (i == 1) {
    // React to i == 1
} else if (i == 2) {
    // React to i == 2
} else if (i == 3) {
    // React to i == 3
} else {
    // Handle every other case
}
```

The alternative in terms of the switch statement is:

Objective-C

```
switch (i) {
    case 1:
        // React to i == 1
        break;
    case 2:
        // React to i == 2
        break;
    case 3:
        // React to i == 3
        break;
    default:
        // Handle every other case
}
```

Two major changes to the way switch works in Swift have greatly enhanced its powers: an ability to switch on more than just integer values, and the ability to employ pattern-matching techniques. Swift also brings a number of smaller changes that make switch statements a little less error-prone than before.

TO INTEGERS AND BEYOND!

While switch statements have always been useful for dealing with integers, if you couldn't boil your data down to numbers, you had to move back to clunkier if constructs, which has long been a source of frustration for developers.

STRINGS

Quite possibly one of the most sought after capabilities is that of being able to match against strings. A common pattern in Objective-C is:

```
if ([stringValue isEqualToString:@"MatchA"]) {
    // Handle for "MatchA"
} else if ([stringValue isEqualToString:@"MatchB"]) {
    // Handle for "MatchB"
} else {
    // Handle for all other possibilities
}
```

Objective-C

Using Swift, this boils down to:

```
switch stringValue {
    case "MatchA":
        // Handle for MatchA
    case "MatchB":
        // Handle for MatchB
    default:
        // Handle for all other possibilities
}
```

Swift

While the length of the two alternatives is not significantly different, the need to state the stringValue variable just once makes refactoring easier and safer, and the Swift code block is arguably easier to comprehend while scanning the code.

ENUMERATIONS

Of course in Objective-C, switching based on the value of an enum is an integral part of development; after all, an Objective-C enum is nothing more than a "coded" integer, and all switch understands is integers.

However, over in the enlightened world of Swift, enumerations are now an object type, and thus no longer have to be plain old integers. We will look at enumerations in detail in Chapter 10, but for now all you need to know is that the underlying value can be as simple as an integer or as complex as a structure, an object, or even nothing at all! Thankfully Swift has you covered.

iOS developers who have worked with table views will be familiar with the UITableViewCellAccessoryType enumeration. If you wanted to check the value of the cell accessory type and perform different behaviors based on the value, you can do the following:

Swift

```swift
var cell = UITableViewCell()
switch cell.accessoryType {
    case UITableViewCellAccessoryType.None: println("None")
    case UITableViewCellAccessoryType.DisclosureIndicator:
    → println("Disclosure Indicator")
    case UITableViewCellAccessoryType.DetailDisclosureButton:
    → println("Disclosure Button")
    case UITableViewCellAccessoryType.Checkmark: println("Checkmark")
    case UITableViewCellAccessoryType.DetailButton: println("Detail Button")
}
```

RANGES

One area in Objective-C where the if statement had the advantage over switch was number ranges. If you wanted to execute different code based on more than individual values, if was your only option. For example:

Objective-C

```objc
NSString *grade;
NSUInteger testScore = getTestScore();
if (testScore >= 0 && testScore < 40) {
    grade = @"F";
} else if (testScore >= 40 && testScore < 60) {
    grade = @"C";
} else if (testScore >= 60 && testScore < 80) {
    grade = @"B";
} else {
    grade = @"A";
}
```

Earlier in this chapter, we looked at the concept of number ranges and in particular the half-open and closed ranges that Swift gives us. Using ranges and a `switch` statement you could easily reimplement this in Swift as:

Swift

```
var testScore = getTestScore()
var grade = ""
switch testScore {
    case 0..<40: grade = "F"
    case 40..<60: grade = "C"
    case 60..<80: grade = "B"
    default: grade = "A"
}
```

You can also use `switch` statements with Swift's other primitive types, including floating point numbers, optionals, and even object types. If you are in doubt about using a type with a `switch` statement, just create a new playground and try it out. And if you're having no luck, there's always pattern matching.

PATTERN MATCHING

In Chapter 3, we briefly covered the pattern match operator (~=) and specifically mentioned that it could be used to great effect with `switch` statements. The pattern match operator is even implicitly added to your conditional statement. There are a number of different pattern types you can match with, and you've already looked at ranges in the previous section. Here, we will examine some more types, including tuples and wildcards, as well as looking at where clauses and value binding.

TUPLES

As you learned in Chapter 3, a tuple is a simple set of ordered data such as a pair of coordinates, a list of places, or a sequence of numbers. Because tuples do not need to be defined in advance, you can assemble them from disparate pieces of data to make complex logic decisions. As an example, consider the following piece of code for customizing `UITableViewCells` based on their position in the table view:

Objective-C

```
if (indexPath.section == 0) {
    // Configuring all cells in section 0 the same way
} else if (indexPath.section == 1) {
    if (indexPath.row == 0) {
        // Configuring cell in row 0 distinct from the rest of section 1
    } else {
        // Configuring remaining cells in section 1 the same way
    }
} else if (indexPath.section == 2) {
```

```
        if (indexPath.row == 3 || indexPath.row == 4 || indexPath.row == 5) {
            // Configuring cells in rows 3, 4, and 5 distinct from rest of section 2
        } else {
            // Configuring remaining cells in section 2 the same way
        }
    } else {
        if (indexPath.row == 0) {
            // Configuring row 0 in any other sections distinct from the rest of
            ↪ the section
        } else {
            // Configuring remaining cells in any other sections the same way
        }
    }
}
```

At the minute, it isn't too hard to follow, but with time and an expanding feature set, this set of nested if statements will start to become harder to read, debug, and maintain. You could reimplement this as a flatter structure using Swift's ability to match on tuples:

Swift

```
switch (indexPath.section, indexPath.row) {
    case (0, 0):
        println("Configuring one row in section 0")
    case (1, 0):
        println("Configuring cell in row 0 distinct from the rest of section 1")
    case (1, 1):
        println("Configuring cell in row 1 distinct from the rest of section 1")
    case (2, 0):
        println("Configuring general cell in section 2")
    case (2, 1):
        println("Configuring general cell in section 2")
    case (2, 2):
        println("Configuring general cell in section 2")
    case (2, 3):
        println("Configuring cells in rows 3, 4, and 5 distinct from rest of
        ↪ section 2")
    case (2, 4):
        println("Configuring cells in rows 3, 4, and 5 distinct from rest of
        ↪ section 2")
    case (2, 5):
        println("Configuring cells in rows 3, 4, and 5 distinct from rest of
        ↪ section 2")
    case (2, 6):
```

```
        println("Configuring general cell in section 2")
    case (3, 0):
        println("Configuring cell in section 3")
    case (4, 0):
        println("Configuring cell in section 3")
}
```

This solution has the advantage of being visually flatter. Unfortunately, it isn't as maintainable; the addition of new rows and sections will require constant updates. The conditional logic of the if statements, and particularly the else blocks, are sorely missing. Luckily there is an answer in the form of wildcards.

WILDCARDS

You first encountered the wildcard pattern very briefly in the previous section on for loops where you used a wildcard to discard the values you were iterating over. The wildcard pattern can also be used with tuples and case statements to match an entire series of entries with one statement. The wildcard operator (_) can be used in any position in the tuples supplied to a case statement, meaning you can match logical groupings like table sections.

Swift

```
switch (indexPath.section, indexPath.row) {
    case (0, _):
        println("Configuring section 0")
    case (1, 0):
        println("Configuring cell in row 0 distinct from the rest of section 1")
    case (1, _):
        println("Configuring remaining cells in section 1 the same way")
    case (2, 3):
        println("Configuring cells in rows 3, 4, and 5 distinct from rest of
          ↪ section 2")
    case (2, 4):
        println("Configuring cells in rows 3, 4, and 5 distinct from rest of
          ↪ section 2")
    case (2, 5):
        println("Configuring cells in rows 3, 4, and 5 distinct from rest of
          ↪ section 2")
    case (2, _):
        println("Configuring remaining cells in section 2 the same way")
    case (_, 0):
        println("Configuring row 0 in any other sections distinct from the rest
          ↪ of the section")
    case (_, _):
        println("Configuring remaining cells in any other sections the same way")
}
```

When using the wildcard operator, bear in mind that if multiple case statements result in a match, the first case is the selected match; if we had placed the last entry (with the double wildcard) anywhere else, it would have a negative impact on the logic. Try to order your case statements from most to least specific, regardless of what type of pattern matching you use!

While this code is more readable, an unfortunate bit of duplication exists in the handling of rows 3, 4, and 5 in section 2. Swift allows you to use ranges in combination with tuples and wildcards. You can refactor the code to a more manageable version by using a range for handling rows 3, 4, and 5. The highlighted line in the following code replaces three case statements:

```swift
switch (indexPath.section, indexPath.row) {
    case (0, _):
        println("Configuring section 0")
    case (1, 0):
        println("Configuring cell in row 0 distinct from the rest of section 1")
    case (1, _):
        println("Configuring remaining cells in section 1 the same way")
    case (2, 3...5):
        println("Configuring cells in rows 3, 4, and 5 distinct from rest of
        → section 2")
    case (2, _):
        println("Configuring remaining cells in section 2 the same way")
    case (_, 0):
        println("Configuring row 0 in any other sections distinct from the rest
        → of the section")
    case (_, _):
        println("Configuring remaining cells in any other sections the same way")
}
```

VALUE BINDINGS

Within conditional statements you often want to have access to the values used to make the decisions. Continuing with the table view cell customization example, you might actually want to know the row and section numbers handled by the wildcard patterns in the last case, the use case being that you want to display the number of the row and section in the cell.

Of course, these values are already available in the form of indexPath.row and indexPath.section, but Swift and UIKit still use the concept of zero-based indexes, which isn't conducive to a good user experience. Creating new values based on the indexPath as part of the case statement block is possible, but you can also use a feature of Swift called *value bindings*; these allow values from the case to be bound to temporary variables or narrowly scoped constants.

You can now rewrite the last case statement to take advantage of value bindings:

Swift

```swift
switch (indexPath.section, indexPath.row) {
    case (0, _):
        println("Configuring section 0")
    case (1, 0):
        println("Configuring cell in row 0 distinct from the rest of section 1")
    case (1, _):
        println("Configuring remaining cells in section 1 the same way")
    case (2, 3...5):
        println("Configuring cells in rows 3, 4, and 5 distinct from rest of
        → section 2")
    case (2, _):
        println("Configuring remaining cells in section 2 the same way")
    case (_, 0):
        println("Configuring row 0 in any other sections distinct from the rest
        → of the section")
    case (var section, let row):
        section++
        println("Configuring cell \(row + 1) in section \(section)")
}
```

By assigning to a variable, you are able to modify the section without worrying about changing the original tuple passed to the switch statement.

Note that the wildcard operators are no longer included in the case statement, but it still retains the same behavior. Think of the wildcard operator as a throwaway variable you do not care about; the value bindings, on the other hand, signify that you are interested in the values they contain.

WHERE CLAUSES

As if using tuples, ranges, and even wildcards didn't give enough flexibility already, Swift adds even more capability by providing the facility to include where clauses in the case statement.

Another common use case when working with table views is the need to place some sort of highlight on a cell to indicate state, often through the use of color or a checkmark disclosure indicator. In our seemingly never-ending example, the sections of the table covered by the last case statement could have a highlight if their index paths are in a separately maintained array of index paths.

You could achieve this using nested conditional statements within the last case. Alternatively, you can make a copy of the case and use a where clause on the first one; remember, you want the case statements to go from most to least specific. A where clause takes a regular conditional expression, and it can use variables and constants from outside the switch statement as well as value bindings from within the case statement itself.

Using a where clause, the code now becomes:

```swift
switch (indexPath.section, indexPath.row) {
    case (0, _):
        println("Configuring section 0")
    case (1, 0):
        println("Configuring cell in row 0 distinct from the rest of section 1")
    case (1, _):
        println("Configuring remaining cells in section 1 the same way")
    case (2, 3...5):
        println("Configuring cells in rows 3, 4, and 5 distinct from rest of
        ➞ section 2")
    case (2, _):
        println("Configuring remaining cells in section 2 the same way")
    case (_, 0):
        println("Configuring row 0 in any other sections distinct from the rest
        ➞ of the section")
    case (var section, let row) where contains(highlightedIndexPaths, indexPath):
        section++
        println("Configuring highlighted cell \(row + 1) in section \(section)")
    case (var section, let row):
        section++
        println("Configuring cell \(row + 1) in section \(section)")
}
```

CUSTOM PATTERN MATCHING

There will always be a use case the developers of Swift cannot foresee, and so they have provided the ability to create custom pattern matching behavior by overloading the pattern match (~=) operator. If you wanted to compare a String object to an Int, or one custom type to another, you will need to supply your own way of comparing the two types. For more information on operator overloading, see Chapter 14.

SAFETY FEATURES

The improvements to switch are not just about usability; the efforts to make Swift a safer programming language have extended to the switch statement as well.

- No fall through by default: This is a fundamental change between the Objective-C and Swift behaviors. If you look at any of the examples in this chapter, you'll notice that none of them feature a break statement. Unlike C and Objective-C, Swift does not allow code to fall through from one case statement to another by default: You have to explicitly request this behavior by adding the fallthrough keyword to the end of your case block. C and

Objective-C developers are often bitten by the accidental omission of a break statement, but this rarely caused an actual error—just time spent debugging strange data problems.

- Multiple conditions can apply to a single case: Now that relying on automatic fall through isn't possible, multiple case conditions can be grouped on one or more lines when separated by commas. If you wanted to match on the values 1, 3, and 5, you can use case 1, 3, 5:. This is more efficient than putting successive lines doing something like the following code sample. This sample is legal but dangerous in Swift—accidentally removing the fallthrough keyword on one line may break a number of conditions.

Swift

```
case 1:
    fallthrough
case 3:
    fallthrough
case 5:
    // Action
```

- The case list must be exhaustive: In Swift, writing a switch statement where none of the supplied case statements are a match isn't possible. If the compiler detects that such a condition has arisen, it reports an error. You can avoid this scenario by ensuring that you create case statements for every possible value, or set of values, by using wildcards or by including a default case.

WRAPPING UP

Given how important control statements are to programming, the major changes in Swift, especially to the switch statement, aren't that surprising. Most of the changes are for the better, and while some may cause a few "style guide" conflicts in the short term, the added safety and convenience in some of the constructs are very welcome.

The next chapter takes a look at optionals—a new feature that has the potential to change some of the code patterns we take for granted and make for more compact and readable source code.

CHAPTER 5
Optionals

An optional differs from a regular variable or constant because it can have two states: It either has some value, or it has no value. When Apple listed the features of their newly announced Swift language, optionals seemed to be one of the concepts that Objective-C developers found the most challenging.

Why? A few possible reasons:

- The misconception that in Objective-C we already have optional variables—assigning `nil` to a pointer is possible, and that makes it an optional, right? Wrong!

- The concept that, for there to be optional variables, there must be non-optional variables as well.

- The very subtle redefinition of the `nil` keyword. In Objective-C, a pointer that has a value of `nil` still has a value, but that value has a coded meaning. In Swift, the `nil` keyword no longer represents that coded value, it means that the variable has *no value*.

- The proliferation of question marks throughout Swift code, making the code look like it has received a visit from The Riddler.

  Whatever the reason, because optionals are being heavily embraced by Apple's frameworks, they are decidedly non-optional.

WHY DO WE NEED OPTIONALS?

When it is first created, an optional has no value (which is represented by `nil`). When you make an assignment that contains a value, the value is stored and is subsequently provided when the optional is used. When you make an assignment of `nil` (no value), the previous value is effectively discarded.

In contrast, a non-optional must always have a value. When created it must be assigned a value that is not `nil`. This may seem unnecessary but has the distinct advantage of allowing us to remove boilerplate code for checking that a value is not `nil`.

Objective-C code is littered with conditional tests to ensure that a pointer is not `nil` before you attempt to use it. Knowing that a variable or constant is a non-optional type means that you can dispense with the `nil`-test and get on with using the value, safe in the knowledge that the compiler would never allow it to be set to `nil`.

Not only that, but when you need to consume third-party APIs and frameworks (even Apple's), you can do so with confidence. If the method definition says that a value returns a non-optional, you can use it without having to worry that it might have no value. Additionally, if an API provider decided to change a method to return an optional, the compiler will detect that you are using an optional as a non-optional and provide an error.

Alternatively if you are the provider of APIs, you can define your own methods to take non-optional values and dispense with the sort of boilerplate code that checks for `nil` parameters being passed.

DECLARING AN OPTIONAL

You can create an optional variant of any type by appending a question mark (?) to the end of its name. Here's how you create an optional variant of an `Int`:

Swift

```
var optional: Int? = 0
```

The question mark is enough to let the compiler, and the maintainers of your code, know that the variable, or constant, can have some value or no value.

USING AN OPTIONAL

Using an optional requires a degree of care, most of which will be forced upon you by the compiler. If you have an optional value and you want to assign it to another optional variable or constant, you can perform a straight assignment:

Swift

```swift
var optional: Int? = 0
var anotherOptional: Int?
anotherOptional = optional
```

Similarly if you wanted to pass it as a parameter to a function that takes an optional as a parameter, you can use it without worrying about whether or not it currently has a value.

However, if you wish to use an optional somewhere that a value is required (for example, in assigning to a non-optional, or calling a method on it), you need to perform some additional work. Unlike Objective-C, where common practice is to send messages to `nil` object pointers, attempting to do likewise in Swift will cause a runtime crash. The Swift compiler makes introducing such crashes much harder, but they are still possible.

UNWRAPPING

So, you've got an optional variable and you want to use it somewhere that expects a non-optional value of the same type. Say, for example, you have an optional `String` variable named `message` you wish to tidy up by ensuring it is properly capitalized. The `String` type has a property named `capitalized` you can use to do this, so you might expect that the following would work:

Swift

```swift
var message: String? = "hi there"
let tidyMessage = message.capitalizedString
```

Unfortunately, the Swift compiler does not like this. It differentiates between the types `String` and `String?`, and unfortunately the optional type does not have a method named `capitalizedString`. In fact optional types generally don't have many methods available to them, and the best thing you can do with an optional is try to get the value out. This is done through a process known as *unwrapping*, and since it is so common in Swift, the developers have provided a shortcut operator to do it quickly.

To unwrap an optional, you use the *forced unwrapping* operator (`!`). Despite using the same character symbol as the logical NOT operator, when unwrapping an optional you place the operator *at the end* of the optional name. As you might expect from the name, when using the forced unwrapping operator, you are telling the Swift compiler you know what you're getting from the optional, and you are confident you can handle the repercussions. Insert the operator at the end of `message` to get access to the underlying `String` value, and then call `capitalizedString` on the result:

Swift

```swift
let message: String? = "hi there"
let tidyMessage = message!.capitalizedString
```

You can think of the forced unwrapping operator as being a shortcut to a method named giveMeYourValueOrGiveMeNil(). But here's the problem: If message is nil, using the forced unwrapping operator is going to return nil, and calling capitalizedString on nil will cause a runtime error. The compiler doesn't protect you here, because you force unwrapped the optional, assuring the compiler you were in control. Try it in a playground by changing the message variable to nil:

```swift
let message: String? = nil
let tidyMessage = message!.capitalizedString
```

Obviously, you need to guard against getting nil back from a forced unwrapping, but how? Fortunately the optional types do respond to the equal and not-equal operators when compared to nil, so you can check if force unwrapping it is safe:

Swift

```swift
let message: String? = nil
var tidyMessage: String?
if message != nil {
    tidyMessage = message!.capitalizedString
}
```

OPTIONAL BINDING

In this simple example, you're using message only once, but in more complicated code, you might want to assign it to a constant scoped within the if block. You could do that like this:

Swift

```swift
if message != nil {
    let definiteMessage = message!
    tidyMessage = definiteMessage.capitalizedString
}
```

Apple recognized that this is likely to become a common pattern, so it added some extra capability to the if and while statements to allow you to perform unwrapping assignments directly within the condition. This technique is known as optional binding and can be performed as follows:

Swift

```swift
if let definiteMessage = message {
    tidyMessage = definiteMessage.capitalizedString
}
```

The assignment operation returns a Boolean that is true if the assignment succeeded (in other words, message contained a value), or false if it didn't. When the assignment succeeds, the newly assigned constant (definiteMessage) is no longer an optional, and can be used safely within the scope of the if block without the need for forced unwrapping. Note that you do not have to assign to a constant and can use a variable instead, but modifying that variable will not have an effect on the original optional value.

IMPLICIT UNWRAPPING

Sometimes you'll have an optional you know will contain a value—for example, you may have assigned a value to it on a previous line. If so, you can take advantage of a feature called *implicit unwrapping*. If you were to assign a value to an optional, say the message variable from the previous example, you could create a special implicitly unwrapped optional that is assumed to have a value. You create this implicitly unwrapped optional as follows:

Swift

```swift
var message: String? = "hi there"
let definiteMessage: String! = message
let tidyMessage = definiteMessage.capitalizedString
```

Again, this is a simple example, but if you needed to use definiteMessage for a number of operations, not needing to force unwrap every time is useful when you know for sure it will be safe. Be careful though—when you use implicit unwrapping you are effectively telling the compiler "it's okay, I got this," and the compiler will leave it up to you. The implicitly unwrapped type (in this example, definiteMessage) has a non-optional type, and if it transpires that the non-optional type has no value, an application can crash at runtime.

OPTIONAL CHAINING

Optional binding is a useful way to test and unwrap an optional safely, but didn't we say that one of the aims of Swift was to reduce the amount of code you needed to write? What happens if you have a number of object types nested within one another and as a result need to nest if statements to delve into the data?

As an (admittedly contrived) example, imagine that you have a UIView hierarchy you wish to traverse from the bottom up. First you'll create your hierarchy:

Swift

```swift
let bottomView = UIView()
let view2 = UIView()
let view3 = UIView()
let view4 = UIView()

view4.addSubview(view3)
view3.addSubview(view2)
view2.addSubview(bottomView)
```

If you were to start at the bottomView and work your way up, the first thing you should do is retrieve its superview property. You would then grab its superview, and its superview. In the world of Objective-C, you can do this very simply:

Objective-C

```objc
UIView *fourthView = bottomView.superview.superview.superview;
```

This takes advantage of Objective-C's ability to send messages to a nil object to make it safe. Because a view is not guaranteed to have a superview, the type of the superview property is UIView?, and the following will not compile:

```swift
let fourthView = bottomView.superview.superview.superview
```

To be safe, you could check by traversing the hierarchy using optional binding:

```swift
if let secondView = bottomView.superview {
    if let thirdView = secondView.superview {
        if let fourthView = thirdView.superview {
            fourthView
        }
    }
}
```

Unfortunately, this is the kind of excessive boilerplate guarding code you want to be doing away with. Swift addresses this through a feature known as *optional chaining.* By using the optional chaining operator (?), applied at the end of an optional property or method call, you can effectively replicate the behavior of sending a message to nil in Objective-C.

A simple way to understand the action of the optional chaining operator is to treat each operator as a decision point; a question as to whether or not to continue. The logic would proceed as follows:

- Calling superview on bottomView returns an optional UIView?.
- If the optional contains no value, the processing finishes, and nil is returned from the overall process.
- If the optional contains a value, superview is called on it, which returns an optional UIView?.
- If this new optional contains no value, the processing finishes, and nil is returned from the overall process.
- If this new optional contains a value, superview is called on it, which returns an optional UIView? from the entire process.

This gives us the following syntax:

```swift
let fourthView = bottomView.superview?.superview?.superview
```

While it doesn't flow quite as smoothly as the Objective-C equivalent, it does remove a lot of extra guarding code. In time, we may even find it favorable due to the presence of the visual indicators of when a nil value may result.

THINGS TO WATCH OUT FOR

Swift developers should be aware of a pair of smaller optional-related considerations that can make dealing with optionals easier: the nil coalescing operator and unwrapping without an operator.

NIL COALESCING OPERATOR

One useful pattern when dealing with optionals is to combine a `nil` check with the ternary conditional operator. When dealing with the `message` example from earlier, you could supply a default value like this:

```Swift
let definiteMessage = message != nil ? message! : "Default"
```

This determines whether `message` is `nil`—if not, it force unwraps `message` and assigns it, otherwise it assigns the string `"Default"`.

This is such a common pattern that the Swift developers have included a shorthand form with its own *nil coalescing operator* (`??`):

```Swift
let definiteMessage = message ?? "Default"
```

Swift is a rapidly evolving language; Apple will continue to identify common usage patterns and seek ways to improve them.

NO NEED TO UNWRAP

We've spent much of this chapter warning you that to use an optional you must always check that it has a value or you risk causing a runtime error. But this isn't always the case. Passing an optional with no value to the `print` or `println` functions does not result in an error. Also, if you use interpolation to embed an optional with no value into a string, you will not see an error.

```Swift
var optionalWithoutValue: String? = nil
```

```
var interpolatedString = "Here comes the optional: \(optionalWithoutValue)!"
```

This code results in a string containing "Here comes the optional: nil!". This is handy because it reduces the amount of optional checking to be done, but at the same time, the lack of consistency throughout the language makes adopting consistent practices harder for us.

WRAPPING UP

Optionals are a simple construct, but they have introduced an additional level of complexity to the language. Like the concept of constants and variables, optionals require forethought to ensure a careful balance between safety and utility. When creating a new constant or variable, or creating a function definition, start off without using an optional, and give yourself the flexibility only when you are sure you need it.

The next chapter continues the explanation of the Swift fundamentals by looking at functions and methods.

CHAPTER 6

Functions

Unless you like to spend most of your time repeating yourself, functions are an essential part of any programming language. Swift functions are a cut above their namesake in Objective-C. A Swift function can be standalone or a method belonging to a class, structure, or enum. They can be created inside another function (known as a *nested function*), can be passed to other functions as parameters, and even returned from functions as a return value. Given their increased importance, saying that functions are now first-class citizens of the Swift world is a fair statement.

In Objective-C, a distinction is made between functions and methods: A function is very much the domain of C code, and methods belong firmly to Objective-C. Their syntax is very different, and as a result saying the words *function* or *method* has clear implications. In Swift there is less of a difference between the two. A method is simply a function belonging to an object type. In this chapter, we use the word *function*, but unless otherwise stated the behaviors described apply to functions whether they are standalone or belong to an object type.

Given the new superpowers of structures and enumerations in Swift, we use the term *object* to refer to any of three types: classes, structures, and enumerations. Similarly the term *instance* will refer to an instantiation of any of these three types. Where necessary, we differentiate the type of object with *class object* or *structure instance*.

CALLING FUNCTIONS

Calling a function in Swift is similar to calling a function in C or C++; just type the name of the function and follow it with parentheses:

Swift
```
functionName()
```

If the function is a method belonging to a class, you can use the dot operator to execute the method on a variable referring to an instance type. If that description sounds complex, it is just because it's needlessly wordy. It looks like this:

Swift
```
instanceVar.methodName()
```

Compare this invocation to Objective-C:

Objective-C
```
[instanceVar methodName];
```

To pass a parameter to a function, put it between the parentheses:

Swift
```
functionName(parameter)
```

If the function takes multiple parameters, they should be comma separated and passed in one of three ways:

- As a plain series of parameters
- As a series of named parameters
- As a combination of both

In the first case, you would make the following call:

Swift
```
functionName(parameter1, parameter2, parameter3)
```

Objective-C has no equivalent to this, and though defining Swift functions this way is possible, you should confine it to circumstances where named parameters provide no useful information to the function's caller.

On the other hand, named parameters are very much an Objective-C feature, and thankfully Swift still supports them. Like Objective-C, you specify the parameter name, follow it with a colon, and then specify the parameter value:

Swift
```
functionName(parameterName1: parameterValue1, parameterName2: parameterValue2)
```

One Swift idiom to be aware of (introduced by the Apple developers themselves) is that the first parameter name is often included in the function name, and is not required in the parameter list. This is actually intended to make the syntax more like Objective-C method calls. For example, consider the following method call in Objective-C:

```
[tableView moveRowAtIndexPath:oldIndexPath toIndexPath:newIndexPath];
```
Objective-C

In Swift this method is called as follows:

```
tableView.moveRowAtIndexPath(oldIndexPath, toIndexPath:newIndexPath)
```
Swift

This makes for much more readable code and is a practice worth adopting when you define your own functions.

DEFINING FUNCTIONS

Defining a Swift function is considerably different from defining an Objective-C method, which uses the following format:

```
- (ReturnType)methodName:(ParameterType1)parameterName1 parameter2:
  (ParameterType2)parameterName2
```
Objective-C

The format for naming Swift functions, however, has the following format:

```
func functionName(paramterName1: ParameterType1, parameterName2:
  ParameterType2) -> ReturnType
```
Swift

All Swift functions must be defined with the keyword func. No—that is not a typo.

PARAMETER NAMING

Swift offers considerable flexibility when naming your function parameters. You can run the gamut from Objective-C's verbosity, all the way to C-style terseness, by choosing whether or not to differentiate between local (or internal) and external parameter names, or to just dispense with parameter names altogether. The best way to demonstrate the options available is to start with the most basic and add verbosity along the way.

UNNAMED PARAMETERS

When we talk about unnamed parameters, bear in mind that *unnamed* means from an external perspective. The parameters still need a local, or internal, name so they can be referenced by the code in the function. To create a function with unnamed parameters, specify the name, a colon, and the type, separating multiple parameters with a comma:

```
func createRectBetweenPoints(firstCorner: CGPoint, secondCorner: CGPoint) {
    let horizontalSize = secondCorner.x - firstCorner.x
    let verticalSize = secondCorner.y - firstCorner.y

    let rect = CGRectMake(firstCorner.x, firstCorner.y,
        horizontalSize, verticalSize)
}
```
Swift

NOTE: This example deliberately does not return the created rectangle to save the nuances of return values until we discuss them.

To use this function, call it as follows:

Swift

```swift
let firstPoint = CGPointMake(0, 0)
let secondPoint = CGPointMake(100, 100)
createRectBetweenPoints(firstPoint, secondPoint)
```

This looks very much like a C function call and is lacking the verbosity we are used to in the Objective-C world. That said, you should write your code the way it suits you, and if there is enough information for you, that's all that matters.

MATCHING NAMED PARAMETERS

If you do want to get more verbose, you need to name the parameters. The simplest way is to use the same name for the local and external parameters. You can do this by placing a hash symbol (# also known as a pound sign, or an octothorpe depending on your particular flavor of English) in front of the parameter names. The function definition becomes:

Swift

```swift
func createRectBetweenPoints(#firstCorner: CGPoint, #secondCorner: CGPoint) {
    let horizontalSize = secondCorner.x - firstCorner.x
    let verticalSize = secondCorner.y - firstCorner.y

    let rect = CGRectMake(firstCorner.x, firstCorner.y, horizontalSize,
    → verticalSize)
}
```

The method call then becomes:

Swift

```swift
createRectBetweenPoints(firstCorner: firstPoint, secondCorner: secondPoint)
```

If you have both these methods in the same playground, you may notice that they can happily co-exist without duplicate function definition errors. Even though they seem almost identical, their different signatures (one has named parameters and one doesn't) mean that they appear different to the compiler.

DIFFERENTIATED NAMED PARAMETERS

One aspect of the naming doesn't seem quite right—you have exposed the local parameter names to the user. Although this is not always a problem, it can be if your internal vocabulary for naming does not make sense to the consumer of your data. In this case, while you're treating these CGPoint instances as corners internally, to the external user you are simply asking for two points.

When defining your functions, you can differentiate between external and local parameter names by stating them in a specific order: *externalName localName: Type*. You can redefine the function as follows:

```swift
func createRectBetweenPoints(firstPoint firstCorner: CGPoint, secondPoint
→ secondCorner: CGPoint) {
    let horizontalSize = secondCorner.x - firstCorner.x
    let verticalSize = secondCorner.y - firstCorner.y

    let rect = CGRectMake(firstCorner.x, firstCorner.y, horizontalSize,
    → verticalSize)
}
```
Swift

Again this new function doesn't clash with the previous two because it has a different signature (the external parameter names are different), and it can be called as follows:

```swift
createRectBetweenPoints(firstPoint: firstPoint, secondPoint: secondPoint)
```
Swift

Of course, it would be a bit more "Objective-C" if you renamed the function to include the first parameter and drop it as an externally named parameter.

```swift
func createRectBetweenFirstPoint(firstCorner: CGPoint, andSecondPoint
→ secondCorner: CGPoint) {
    let horizontalSize = secondCorner.x - firstCorner.x
    let verticalSize = secondCorner.y - firstCorner.y

    let rect = CGRectMake(firstCorner.x, firstCorner.y, horizontalSize,
    → verticalSize)
}
```
Swift

And to call it:

```swift
createRectBetweenFirstPoint(firstPoint, andSecondPoint: secondPoint)
```
Swift

The concept of externally named parameters being different from the local parameters may seem a bit strange, but we've long been using similar constructs in Objective-C where we often embed external names for parameters in the selector. This is how we've been able to use such expressive selector names, giving our code the readability for which it is often noted.

DEFAULT PARAMETER VALUES

C++ or Objective-C++ users will be familiar with the concept of default parameter values. When defining a function, you can specify a value that should be used within the function body if the calling code does not pass a value for it. This can be a benefit when writing code that has a number of commonly used parameters that might only need to be deviated from on occasion.

For example, consider the following Objective-C method for creating a URL from domain, path, and protocol components:

```objectivec
+ (NSString *)createUrlStringForDomain:(NSString *)domain withPath:(NSString *)
→ path andProtocol:(NSString *)proto {
    return [NSString stringWithFormat:@"%@://%@/%@", proto, domain, path];
}
```
Objective-C

The protocol is often "http" and the path is often an empty string, so creating convenience methods that allow the protocol, or the protocol and path, to be omitted is useful:

Objective-C

```
+ (NSString *)createUrlStringForDomain:(NSString *)domain withPath:
→ (NSString *)path
    return [self createUrlStringForDomain:domain path:path andProtocol:
    → @"http"];
}
```

Objective-C

```
+ (NSString *)createUrlStringForDomain:(NSString *)domain {
    return [self createUrlStringForDomain:domain withPath:@""];
}
```

This is a perfect example of where default parameter values could be used to great effect. To define a default value, add an assignment into the parameter definition in the function definition:

Swift

```
func createUrlStringForDomain(domain: String, withPath path: String =
→ "", andProtocol proto: String = "http") -> String {
    return "\(proto)://\(domain)/\(path)"
}
```

With just this one function definition, you can call this method in three different ways:

- `let swiftBlogUrl = createUrlStringForDomain("developer.apple.com",
  withPath: "swift/blog", andProtocol: "https")`
- `let bbcNewsUrl = createUrlStringForDomain("www.bbc.co.uk", withPath: "news")`
- `let googleUrl = createUrlStringForDomain("www.google.com")`

If you define a parameter with a default value and no external parameter name, Swift will provide one for you. The Swift developers believe that default parameters should be named to make their purpose clear. If you strongly disagree, you can specify an external parameter name of _ to suppress this behavior.

RETURN VALUES

So far we haven't really delved too deeply into the subject of return values. Like Objective-C, functions in Swift can either return a single type, or they can return nothing. However, by returning a tuple, you can effectively return as many values as you wish; this is a great additional feature, but it should be used with caution. Overusing the ability to return a tuple may make your code harder to understand and maintain.

When defining a function that should return a value, you need to type a *return arrow* (->) after the closing parenthesis (round bracket) of the parameter list, and then specify the type of the value you want your function to return. There are a few variations on this form:

- `func functionName()` has no return value.
- `func functionName() -> ()` returns an empty tuple, the same as no return value.

- `func functionName() -> Void` returns an empty tuple, as Void is a type alias for ().
- `func functionName() -> Int` returns an integer type.
- `func functionName() -> Int?` returns an optional integer type.
- `func functionName() -> (Int, String)` returns a two-value tuple where the values are unnamed.
- `func functionName() -> (Int, String)?` returns an optional two-value tuple; the tuple may or may not exist.
- `func functionName() -> (anInt: Int, aString: String)` returns a two-value tuple where the values are named.

In the previous section, you defined the functions without a return type to keep focused on the parameter naming. The obvious omission was to return the CGRect you actually created:

Swift

```swift
func createRectBetweenFirstPoint(firstCorner: CGPoint, andSecondPoint
→ secondCorner: CGPoint) -> CGRect {
    let horizontalSize = secondCorner.x - firstCorner.x
    let verticalSize = secondCorner.y - firstCorner.y

    let rect = CGRectMake(firstCorner.x, firstCorner.y, horizontalSize,
    → verticalSize)
    return rect
}
```

Note that you can again define this function in addition to the other that shares the same name. This is because the signature of the two functions is differentiated by the return type.

MODIFYING FUNCTION PARAMETERS

When you pass a parameter to a function, it's treated as a constant by default. Attempting to modify the parameter will result in a compiler error:

Swift

```swift
func canWeChangeItNoWeCant(constantParam: Int) {
    constantParam = 0
}
```

You can modify parameters within the body of a function in two ways: Mark them as variable parameters or as in-out parameters.

VARIABLE PARAMETERS

Swift treats passed parameters as constants by default. These constants follow the same rules as those you create using the `let` keyword. You can explicitly mark a parameter as a constant using the `let` keyword if you so desire, but it will probably result in a lot of extra typing for an assumption that many people will make anyway.

To make the parameter in the previous example modifiable, all you need to do is explicitly mark the parameter as a variable using the var keyword. In doing so, the error caused by trying to modify the parameter will go away:

Swift

```
func canWeChangeItYesWeCan(var variableParam: Int) {
    variableParam = 0
}
```

This behavior has two things worth noting. First, this is the same behavior exhibited by Objective-C. It may seem strange that, in Swift, the default is for passed parameters to be constants, while Objective-C allows the user to modify a variable by default. Again, this boils down to safety. In Objective-C a developer can inadvertently make a change to a passed parameter without realizing it, affecting the use of that parameter later in the function. In Swift, this isn't possible without intentionally marking a parameter as a variable.

Second, marking a parameter as a variable does not propagate any changes made back to the original value passed in to the function. To do that, you need to use in-out parameters.

IN-OUT PARAMETERS

A common pattern in Objective-C code is passing a pointer to a pointer as another way to get information back to the calling code. This is most familiar within Cocoa and Cocoa Touch methods that need to provide an NSError back to the calling code, as well as data relating to the method; the data is passed back as the return value, and information about any errors encountered is populated into an NSError object.

Objective-C (or more accurately, C) does this through pointers: To pass back a primitive, you need to pass a pointer to a primitive to the function or method, and to pass back an object pointer, you need to pass back a pointer to an object pointer. This requires careful definition of a function or method, and in calling as well. It is easy to get wrong, and isn't a particularly user-friendly aspect of the language.

To make Swift more modern, the developers included a keyword named inout to use in a function parameter definition to indicate that the parameter passed into the function can also be modified. For example, the following function modifies the value of an integer, but also returns true or false to indicate success or failure:

Swift

```
func doubleThisInt(inout intToChange: Int) -> Bool {
    intToChange *= 2
    return true
}
```

Allowing any value to be changed by a function that takes an in-out parameter would be quite dangerous, especially when consuming a third-party framework. Between revisions, the framework provider could change a harmless function to start modifying values. To combat this, Swift retains some vestiges of its C heritage by mandating that in-out parameters must be passed with a leading ampersand (&), otherwise compilation will fail. This gives a clue to the original developer writing the code that they are about to pass a value into a function that will modify the value, and also to code maintainers who are trying to understand it later.

To call the doubleThisInt function, you would use this:

Swift

```swift
var intToChange = 2
var success = doubleThisInt(&intToChange)
println("Doubled int: \(intToChange)")
```

We look at working with Objective-C frameworks that take pointers to object pointers (such as the NSError pattern) in more detail in Chapter 14.

VARIADIC PARAMETERS

A *variadic* parameter takes an unspecified number of values. We use these as consumers a lot in Objective-C, particularly when using the stringWithFormat: pattern for string construction, or even with NSLog, but we tend to use them a lot less as producers. That may be because parsing variadic parameter lists in Objective-C is not as intuitive as it could be (it's all based around C functions).

As an example, consider a method intended to take a sequence of characters that will be used to build a string. (It's not a particularly practical example, but it's still an example.) In Objective-C, you need to provide a method definition that includes a variadic parameter, and in the method body you need to initialize (using va_start) and parse the variadic argument list (using the va_arg function), and remember to close the list afterwards (va_end):

Objective-C

```objc
+ (NSString *)stringFromCharacters:(BOOL)forward, ... {
    NSMutableString * outputString = [NSMutableString stringWithFormat:@""];
    va_list variableArgs;
    va_start(variableArgs, forward);
    for (NSString * character = va_arg(variableArgs, NSString * );
    → character != nil; character = va_arg(variableArgs, NSString * )) {
        if (forward) {
            [outputString appendString:character];
        } else {
            NSMutableString * mutableCharacter = [character mutableCopy];
            [mutableCharacter appendString:outputString];
            outputString = mutableCharacter;

        }
    }
    va_end(variableArgs);

    return [outputString copy];
}
```

Note that in C and Objective-C, you can create a variadic parameter list only if you have at least one regular parameter type as well. To use this method, you need to call it as follows:

Objective-C

```
NSString *output = [NSString stringFromCharacters:YES, @"a", @"b", @"c", nil];
```

You had to use a `nil`-terminated list so that the processing can stop at some stage; you could avoid this by specifying how many parameters you are passing, or having some way of detecting the number to be passed (for example, by parsing a formatting string).

Swift makes a number of improvements to the use of variadic parameters. When defining the variadic parameter list, you can specify a name, and the type of parameters. You are not forced to have at least one regular parameter before the variadic list.

Inside the function body, you have access to an array corresponding to the type specified in the definition, which you can iterate over using a standard `for-in` loop. This makes for a more modern syntax and more easily comprehended code, and removes the need for tracking the parameter count—no need to worry about passing parameter counts or using sentinel values like `nil`.

Swift

```
func stringFromCharacters(forward: Bool, characters: Character...) -> String {
    var outputString: String = ""
    for character in characters {
        if (forward) {
            outputString = outputString + String(character)
        } else {
            outputString = String(character) + outputString
        }
    }
    return outputString
}
```

```
let outputString = stringFromCharacters(true, "a", "b", "c")
```

Using variadic parameters still has some restrictions:

- You can use only one per function—otherwise you wouldn't be able to tell when one parameter list ended and the next began.
- It must appear at the end of the parameter list, which prevents confusion about what is a variadic parameter and what is a regular parameter.
- If you use a named parameter for the variadic function, it must be included only once in the calling code.
- If you have default parameter values, you must place the variadic parameter after the last default value. If you take advantage of a default value, you cannot pass any values to the variadic parameter (it will be an empty array).

FUNCTION SCOPES

The data accessible to a function is dependent on its scope and the data passed in as parameters.

GLOBAL SCOPE

Functions defined at the global scope have access to the global data of the application. Because Swift has no distinct header and implementation files, a variable, constant, or function defined outside a data structure belongs to the global scope, and can be used from any other source file.

SCOPE OF METHODS

Although we have yet to discuss methods (covered in Chapters 9 and 10), a method is simply a function associated with an object type such as a class, structure, or enumeration. A method has access to all the member data associated with the object type as well as data at the global scope.

NESTED FUNCTIONS

A nested function is defined inside another function. Nested functions behave mostly the same, but have some interesting properties. In the same way that a global function has access to the global scope, the nested function has access to the scope of the function in which it is defined (as well as the global scope, and member data if the function is an object method). Any variables or constants defined in that scope become available within the nested function.

A nested function can be executed only from within the scope of the function within which it is defined. The exception to this is when the nested function is passed out of the defining function as a return value to the calling code. We cover the returning of functions in the next section.

The following code sample shows an outer function with a nested inner function:

```swift
func outerFunction() {
    var outerVariable = 0

    func innerFunction() {
        outerVariable++
    }
    innerFunction()
    innerFunction()
    innerFunction()

    println(outerVariable)
}
```

Swift

When the `outerFunction` is executed, it sets up the integer variable and defines `inner-Function`. The `innerFunction` has access to the variable, and each time it is called, the variable is incremented. When printed, the value of the variable will be 3.

USING FUNCTIONS

In Swift, functions have become their own type, which is a major difference between Swift and Objective-C. This might seem like an inconsequential difference, but it means that the line between functions and Objective-C blocks (called *closures* in Swift) is blurred.

Although in Objective-C, functions may never have had their own type, you could always use function pointers to achieve something similar, but being a feature of the C language it has always felt not very Objective-C-like. Function pointers also held no type information; you had a pointer to a function, and the caller had to be aware of what parameters to pass and what would be returned.

The native Objective-C alternative would be to use methods from the `performSelector:` family. While these are useful, they are limited to being able to pass zero or one parameters with a text-based selector to a specific object. It's no surprise that blocks have become an exceptionally popular replacement when this kind of functionality is required.

FUNCTION TYPES

Swift function types are not only a first-class citizen of the language, but they have the function's own type information as an integral part of the type. A function's type information is derived from the combination of its parameter types and its return type. Consider the following function definition:

Swift

```swift
func isNumberSameAsString(number: Int, string: String) -> Bool {
    return "\(number)" == string
}
```

The type for a function is stated using the format: *(parameter types) -> (return type)*. For the function above, the function type would be:

Swift

```swift
(Int, String) -> (Bool)
```

If a function has no parameters or no return type, use empty parentheses:

Swift

```swift
() -> ()
```

A function can be stored by assigning it to a constant or variable:

Swift

```swift
let numberFunction = isNumberSameAsString
```

The parentheses are not added when storing a function—including them would make this a call to the function instead. To use a stored function, call it as you normally would, but use the stored name in place of the function name.

```Swift
numberFunction(350125, "350125")
```

When using function types, be aware that a function with external parameter names can affect the inferred function type. For example, if you were to adjust the original function definition to be:

```Swift
func isNumber(number: Int, sameAsString string: String) -> Bool {
    return "\(number)" == string
}
```

you can assign this to a variable or constant in three different ways:

- `let unspecifiedNumberFunction = isNumber`
- `let explicitNumberFunction: (Int, sameAsString: String) -> (Bool) = isNumber`
- `let generalNumberFunction: (Int, String) -> (Bool) = isNumber`

The parameter name can be explicitly stated as part of the type. Explicitly stating the parameter name (`explicitNumberFunction`), or just letting type inference (`unspecifiedNumberFunction`) do the work, means that the function can be called only by including the parameter name. Defining the function type without the external parameter name (`generalNumberFunction`) allows the function to be called without the external parameter name.

```Swift
unspecifiedNumberFunction(1, sameAsString: "1")
explicitNumberFunction(2, sameAsString: "2")
generalNumberFunction(3, "3")
```

Having the external parameter names within your function types may be more trouble than it is worth; specifying a more general type allows functions with different external parameter names to be used in the same places. This is much more useful for passing functions around or storing them as member data in object types. If you plan on using function types extensively, using a type alias to define the type in a more descriptive way may be useful:

```Swift
typealias numberToStringComparisonType = (Int, String) -> (Bool)
```

```
let typedNumberFunction: numberToStringComparisonType = isNumber
typedNumberFunction(4, "4")
```

This all may seem a bit pointless. Why call a function using an alternative name when the original function name is still available to call directly? Because it *is* pointless—the real power in function types comes when they are passed to and returned from other functions.

USING FUNCTIONS AS PARAMETER VALUES

To pass a function to another function, the function type needs to be stated as a parameter in the new function definition. To pass the isNumberSameAsString function (that we defined in the previous section) to another function, you would use:

Swift

```
func compareNumber(number: Int, toString string: String,
→ withComparator comparator: (Int, String) -> (Bool)) -> Bool {
    return comparator(number, string)
}
```

The function definition is starting to get a bit punctuation heavy, which is where a good type alias can come in handy:

Swift

```
func compareNumber(number: Int, toString string: String,
→ withComparator comparator: numberToStringComparisonType) -> Bool {
    return comparator(number, string)
}
```

To use a function as a parameter, just pass it in by name:

Swift

```
compareNumber(5, toString: "5", withComparator: generalNumberFunction)
```

USING FUNCTIONS AS RETURN VALUES

The ability to return functions from other functions allows you to write code that defers the decisions on which functions to call to another function. Say you introduced a new number comparison that worked "back to front" (by converting the string to an integer instead of the other way around):

Swift

```
func compareStringToNumber(number: Int, string: String) -> Bool {
    if let convertedInt = string.toInt() {
        return number == convertedInt
    } else {
        return false
    }
}

compareNumber(6, toString: "6", withComparator: compareStringToNumber)
```

You now have two comparator functions to choose from, so you can make an overall decision as to which one to use based on a Boolean value:

```swift
func compareNumber(number: Int, toString string:String, forwards:Bool) -> Bool {
    if (forwards) {
        return compareNumber(number, toString: string, withComparator:
          → isNumberSameAsString)
    } else {
        return compareNumber(number, toString: string, withComparator:
          → compareStringToNumber)
    }
}
```

Some duplication here could be abstracted out. The forwards value can be passed to a function that returns the appropriate comparator in response. Returning a function requires that a function type be specified as the return type. Note that this produces what looks like an "extra" return type, which may look strange:

```swift
func selectComparator(forwards: Bool) -> ((Int, String) -> (Bool)) {
    if (forwards) {
        return isNumberSameAsString
    } else {
        return compareStringToNumber
    }
}
```

With this in place, the compareNumber function can be reduced to:

```swift
func compareNumber(number: Int, toString string:String, forwards:Bool) -> Bool {
    let comparator = selectComparator(forwards)
    return compareNumber(number, toString: string, withComparator: comparator)
}
```

WRAPPING UP

As with any language, functions (and methods) form one of the core approaches by which code can be broken down into manageable chunks and reused. Underneath the seemingly basic syntax, which looks like a combination of various scripting languages, C++, and Java, lies a powerful and complex set of features that promote safety and modernity over the familiarity of Objective-C.

In the next chapter, we will look at closures, Swift's equivalent to blocks.

CHAPTER 7
Blocks and Closures

Blocks are a relatively new addition to iOS and OS X development, and although Apple delivered them as part of Objective-C, they are actually an enhancement to the C language itself. This comes through in their syntax: It is confusing, hard to remember, and unintuitive. Any syntax that inspires developers to create websites like Gosh Darn Block Syntax (http://goshdarnblocksyntax.com) as a blocks cheat sheet cannot be considered to be particularly user friendly.

Despite this, blocks are here to stay, and they're taking over our APIs. Apple took the time to improve the syntax of blocks, and to provide numerous syntactical optimizations that simplify their usage in many common patterns. They also decided to rename blocks, giving them a more modern name—closures—that has more in common with the names of their counterpart functionality in many other languages and reduces the potential for confusion when talking about simple blocks of code.

DEFINING CLOSURES

Objective-C's blocks and Swift's closures are similar in that they can be used in a number of ways. While they can be passed as parameters to, and returned from, methods, they can also be defined and used inline, requiring a less formal syntax for creation and use. This is where the syntax confusion starts to arise with blocks, and where closures seek to simplify matters.

CREATING THE DEFINITION

The first experience most developers have with blocks is when they need to pass one into an existing method, often a UIKit or AppKit API. Because these are easily handled inline in the method call, they can be thought of as anonymous blocks; they don't exist anywhere but in the method call. This reduces the complexity of the syntax a little, and they boil down to the following general format:

Objective-C
```
[object methodName:^ReturnType(ParamType1 paramName1, ParamType2 paramName2,
→ ...) {
    // Code within the block
}];
```

Consider a method that receives a block, which takes two NSString parameters and returns an NSString:

Objective-C
```
[greetingMaker produceGreeting:^NSString *(NSString *format, NSString *name) {
    return [NSString stringWithFormat:format, name];
}];
```

Bearing in mind that this is the *simplest* way to use a block, it seems natural that Apple would seek to simplify the process somewhat for closures. To pass a closure as a parameter to a function or method, you can use this syntax:

Swift
```
object.methodName( { (paramName1: ParamType1, paramName2: ParamType2) ->
→ (ReturnType) in
    // Code within the closure
} )
```

This syntax may seem familiar, because it is almost identical to that used for defining a function or method. The only deviation is the use of the in keyword, which is intended to indicate that the defined parameters should be used *in* the following code statements. And best of all, you don't have to remember where to stick the caret (^)! Our earlier produce-Greeting example becomes slightly simpler in Swift:

Swift
```
greetingMaker.produceGreeting( { (format: String, name: String) -> (String) in
    return NSString(format:format, name)
} )
```

ASSIGNING TO VARIABLES

The inline creation of blocks is often the first place Objective-C developers get to grips with the syntax. Yet just when they feel they've learned it, along comes the next challenge: defining a variable to assign a block to. Unfortunately the caret position and parentheses' use varies, which makes remembering their placement difficult:

```
ReturnType (^blockVariableName)(ParamType1 paramName1, ParamType2 paramName2,
→ ...);
```
Objective-C

So if you wanted to create a reference to a block for later use with the produceGreeting method, you would define a variable as follows:

```
NSString * (^greetingMaker)(NSString *, NSString *);
```
Objective-C

To create a closure variable in Swift requires the following general syntax:

```
var closureVariableName: (ParamType1, ParamType2, ...) -> (ReturnType)
```
Swift

The Swift syntax is very easy to remember given just how similar it is to a regular function or method definition. It becomes even easier when combined with type inference if you assign a closure to the variable at the same time:

```
var closureVariableName = { (paramName1: ParamType1, paramName2: paramType2,
→ ...) -> ReturnType in
   // code within the closure
}
```
Swift

To create and assign a closure to a variable for this example becomes:

```
var greetMaker = { (format: String, name: String) -> (String) in
    return NSString(format:format, name)
}
```
Swift

RECEIVING AS FUNCTION PARAMETERS

Another place where blocks are defined is as parameters passed to methods, as well as return values. Once again, the syntax varies and becomes yet another source of frustration to the Objective-C developer:

```
- (MethodReturnType)methodName:(BlockReturnType(^)(ParamType1, ParamType2,
→ ...))blockParamName;
```
Objective-C

Creating a method definition for the produceGreeting method results in:

```
- (NSString *)produceGreeting:(NSString *(^)(NSString *, NSString *))
→ greetingMaker;
```
Objective-C

Thankfully, the Swift syntax for using a closure type as a parameter is the same as it is elsewhere:

```
func methodName(closureParamName: (ParamType1, ParamType2, ...) ->
→ (ClosureReturnType)) -> MethodReturnType { }
```

This makes our produceGreeting method definition:

```
func produceGreeting(greetingMaker: (String, String) -> (String)) ->
→ String { ... }
```

CREATING TYPE ALIASES

One technique used in Objective-C to reduce the complexity of block type definitions is to use typedefs to simplify the types. This is a useful practice although it comes with yet another syntax and has some of its own drawbacks. Without being well-named, the typedefs can hide the actual behavior of the block itself. To create a typedef for a block type:

```
typedef ReturnType(^BlockTypeName)(ParamType1, ParamType2, ...);
```

You can make a GreetingMakerType and instantiate it like this:

```
typedef NSString *(^GreetingMakerType)(NSString *, NSString *);
GreetingMakerType greetingMaker;
```

In Swift, you can take advantage of type aliases to achieve a similar effect:

```
typealias ClosureTypeName = (ParamType1, ParamType2, ...) -> (ReturnType)
```

You can make a GreetingMakerType and use it in the produceGreeting definition as follows:

```
typealias GreetingMakerType = (String, String) -> String
func produceGreeting(greetingMaker: GreetingMakerType) -> String { ... }
```

EXECUTING CLOSURES

Actually executing a closure is very much the same as executing a block in Objective-C—call it like a standalone function:

```
returnValue = closureVariableName(paramName1: param1, paramName2: param2, ...)
```

To execute the greetMaker closure you created earlier, you would do this:

```
let greeting = greetMaker("Hello, %@!", "World")
```

One pattern you see a lot in Objective-C is performing a not-nil test on a block variable before use:

```
if (blockVariable != nil) {
    blockVariable();
}
```

You can reduce the need for this type of guarding in Swift through careful use of non-optional types. If a variable, constant, or function parameter is not an optional value, it can never be `nil` and is safe to execute directly. If it is an optional, optional binding also works with block values.

OPTIMIZING CLOSURES

Even though Apple made general improvements to the syntax for closures, you can still employ several techniques to streamline the inline closure definitions, both in isolation and in combination.

IMPLICIT RETURNS

When a closure body consists of a single return statement, the Swift compiler can infer the return keyword when it is omitted:

```
greetMaker = { (format: String, name: String) -> (String) in
    NSString(format:format, name)
}
```
Swift

Here, the compiler knows that this closure will return a string, so it adds the return on your behalf.

TYPE INFERENCE

Type inference can also be used within a closure to infer the passed parameter types.

```
greetMaker = { format, name in
    NSString(format:format, name)
}
```
Swift

In this case, the types for format and name, as well as the return type, are inferred from the variable greetMaker; it already specifies that it is a closure that takes two strings and returns a string. The parentheses surrounding the parameter names can also be omitted.

SHORTHAND ARGUMENT NAMES

Another optimization comes in the form of shorthand argument names. If you are already using type inference, the only information before the in keyword is the names of the parameters. By instead referring to them as generic indexed parameter names ($0, $1, and so on), you can freely omit the parameter names and the in keyword:

```
greetMaker = {
    NSString(format:$0, $1)
}
```
Swift

The value of this optimization is up for debate. The reduction in boilerplate code is certainly welcome, but if your closure code is particularly complex, you may wish to keep the names of the parameters intact to enhance readability.

TRAILING CLOSURE SYNTAX

When passing a closure as the last, or only, parameter to a function, Swift allows you to take the closure outside the normal parentheses for the function. This is especially helpful when a closure consists of a significant amount of code and makes for better readability and maintainability:

Swift

```
greetingMaker.produceGreeting() {
    NSString(format: $0, $1);
}
```

NOTE: If the function takes parameters other than the closure, it must be the last parameter in the list. The remaining parameters must still be placed with the parentheses.

OPERATOR FUNCTIONS

In what might be considered by some to be an optimization too far, the Swift developers have opted to allow the following as valid syntax:

```
match = pair.matches(==)
```

To understand how we got here, consider the following structure (we'll explain the details about structures in Chapter 10) that represents a pair of items, such as cards in a matching pairs game:

Swift

```
struct Pair {
    var first:String, second:String
    func matches( comparison:(String, String) -> Bool) -> Bool {
        return comparison(first, second)
    }
}
let pair = Pair(first: "Swift", second: "Swift")
```

The structure is created with two strings (here they are both "Swift"), and it contains a function named matches that compares the two strings using a supplied closure. This allows users of the code to supply their own "matching algorithm":

Swift

```
var match = pair.matches({ (left: String, right: String) -> Bool in
    return left == right
})
```

Using some of the optimizations detailed in the previous sections, you can reduce this down quite significantly:

Swift

```
match = pair.matches({ left, right in        // Inferred types
    return left == right
})
match = pair.matches({ return $0 == $1 })    // Shorthand argument names
match = pair.matches({ $0 == $1 })           // Implicit return
```

This results in a nice compact syntax, but if you were beginning to worry that Swift wasn't truly obfuscation-friendly, you can relax. Another optimization is *operator functions*: When your closure types match those of an operator (in this case a string compared to a string and returning a Boolean), you can substitute the operator in place of the rest of the closure body.

Swift

```
match = pair.matches(==)
```

Now that you know this feature exists, please try to forget about it (for the sake of the people who have to maintain your code).

CAPTURING VALUES

The reason closures are so named is because they can "close over" or capture values from their enclosing scope—a behavior they share with blocks in Objective-C.

The only significant difference between Swift and Objective-C is Swift's lack of a __block modifier. In Objective-C, any value captured by and modified within a block must be marked with the __block modifier, which indicates to the compiler the value should be captured by reference and not just copied by value into the block's scope.

The Objective-C compiler is intelligent enough to detect when you modify a captured value and flag it as an error, indicating that you should add the __block modifier to the captured variable so it can be captured by reference. The Swift compiler goes one step further and does this on your behalf, automatically capturing by reference when necessary. The only downside is that you lose the visual cues as to which variables are intended to be modified in the closure.

WRAPPING UP

The underlying power and flexibility of blocks has not changed significantly in the transformation to closures in Swift. What has changed is their ease of use. The syntax is more consistent among the various ways of defining and using closures, and it is also consistent with that used for functions and methods. The next chapter examines Swift's native string support, replicating common NSString operations and interacting with NSString where necessary.

CHAPTER 8

Strings

Strings are a core component of any programming language. Until the day we can program, and interact, with our computers completely through verbal and audio cues, text will continue to be our primary method of interfacing with these machines. Most other programming languages have sufficiently advanced native string support, yet surprisingly Objective-C relies on Apple's Foundation library to provide anything more advanced than the low-level string functions provided by C.

Swift's powerful native string type (conveniently named `String`) is designed to coexist with `NSString`. Given the extent to which `NSString` is embedded in the AppKit and UIKit frameworks, being able to use `String` wherever an `NSString` is expected (and vice versa) is somewhat of a relief.

Strings in Swift are implemented as a structure, and the underlying representation is that of a collection of `Character` values. Unlike Objective-C where a `char` is a single byte of data, a Swift `Character` is a genuine Unicode character and as a result the `String` type handles Unicode natively as well.

CONSTRUCTING STRINGS

Given the importance of strings to any programming language, Swift strings naturally have their own literal syntax for creation and usage. As an object type, String does have an init method you can use as a constructor, but seeing a string created in this way is unusual.

```
let initString = String.init("By init")
let constructorString = String("By constructor")
let literalString = "By literal syntax"
```

Unlike NSString, the Swift string can be easily built from smaller strings by concatenating with the addition operator (+). Although some people disagree with using the concept of "adding strings" to represent concatenation, it is a pattern used in enough programming languages to be immediately understood by many developers.

```
let concatenatedString = "Hello, " + "World!"
```

Like in other modern languages, creating strings from constants or variables can easily be done using string interpolation. No formatting strings, like those used by NSString, are necessary; Swift provides a direct interpolation syntax. To include a variable or constant in your string, prefix the name with a backslash and an opening parenthesis, and suffix the name with a closing parenthesis:

```
let entity = "World"
let interpolatedString = "Hello, \(entity)!"
```

NOTE: The actual value included in the string is the output of the description method called on the variable or constant being interpolated into the string.

As well as constructing from existing strings, a String can also be created from the Character type. To create a single character string, use the version of the initializer that takes a Character:

```
let character: Character = "="
let characterString = String(character)
```

String also has convenience methods for creating a string from a single repeated character. For example, if you needed to create a dividing line effect in your application's log file, you could create a 20 character–long string of equals signs like this:

```
let dividingLine = String(count: 20, repeatedValue: character)
```

MANIPULATING STRINGS

Interacting with strings you've created, or that you've received from APIs and frameworks, is fundamental to much of OS X and iOS development. These interactions can be divided into three groups: examining, comparing, and modifying.

EXAMINING STRING VALUES

Many operations involving strings in Swift require using an index that points to a specific character in the string, or an index range that indicates a contiguous sequence of characters. Many of the NSString methods take a similar approach to string manipulation with one extremely important difference: In NSString the index, or range, is based on an integer value, whereas in Swift it is not.

We have already remarked that a Swift string is based on a collection of Character values, the size of which can vary depending on the content of the character. In NSString, passing a plain integer index of n to a string manipulation method indicates that the method should operate at the character n bytes from the start of the string. Trying to do the same with a Swift string could result in a method trying to perform a manipulation on the wrong character, or worse still, between two bytes of a multibyte character.

To deal with this issue, Swift string methods do not take a plain integer as an index, but instead take an instance of a String.Index, provided by the string itself. This index can be safely traversed by calling functions on it, effectively allowing the user to manipulate strings in terms of characters instead of bytes.

Each string provides two basic indexes through properties: startIndex and endIndex. When these are requested, they are created to point to the start and end of the string, respectively.

The String type supports subscript notation, so you can retrieve a single character by supplying a valid String.Index value. For example:

```Swift
var string = "string"
var index = string.startIndex
var character = string[index]
```

To move the index along the string, use the advance function by passing it a String.Index and an Int representing the number of characters to advance by. To retrieve the second character, advance the index by 1:

```Swift
index = advance(index, 1)
let secondCharacter = string[index]
```

To move backward, pass a negative value to the advance function, and to work backward from the end of the string, use the endIndex as your starting point. Bear in mind that endIndex refers to the *end* of the string, after the last character. To get the last character, you need to "advance" by –1, to get the second-to-last, "advance" by –2, and so on.

```
index = string.endIndex
index = advance(index, -2)
let secondLastCharacter = string[index]
```

Be careful with String.Index values. Indexes are tied to the string they are retrieved from, and using an index from one string to access the contents of another is dangerous. Furthermore, attempting to advance an index beyond the end of the string will cause a runtime error. You can use a variant of advance that takes an end parameter, which will stop the index being advanced beyond the index specified in the end parameter. If you have any concerns you may advance too far, use this variant, and use a suitable end index. If you're not sure what to use, you can always use the index of the last character, which you can get by "advancing" one character *backward* from the endIndex:

```
index = advance(string.startIndex, 7, advance(string.endIndex, -1))
```

The Swift String type does not have a length property similar to that provided by NSString, but it can be used with the Swift standard library function countElements. This returns the number of characters in a string, but bear in mind that this is not an indicator of the number of bytes required to store the string.

```
let stringLength = countElements(string)
```

You may be tempted to try combining the advance function and knowledge of a string's length to iterate over its characters, but there is no need. The Swift String type conforms to the SequenceType protocol, which means you can iterate the characters using a for-in loop:

```
for character in string {
    print(character)
}
```

COMPARING STRINGS

String comparison is an important facet of any modern programming language. Whether you used NSString or C strings, you've probably made some sort of error when trying to compare two strings in Objective-C. Using the equals operator (==) to compare two NSString objects seems like a reasonable assumption, or that the positive result of strcmp should not be 0, but at some stage we've all found out that it is a wrong assumption.

Thankfully, the Swift developers recognized some of these problems, and string comparison in Swift is reasonably straightforward. The equals operator can be used to compare two strings, returning true or false as appropriate:

```
let string1 = "string"
let string2 = "strong"
let string3 = "string"

string1 == string2     // returns false
string1 == string3     // returns true
```

Naturally, the not equals operator (!=) also works as you would expect:

```Swift
string1 != string2      // returns true
```

> **NOTE:** The ability to directly compare two strings using the equals operator makes string comparisons an extremely useful enhancement to Swift's supercharged switch statement. If you use a lot of string comparisons in a single if conditional, consider using switch.

The less-than (<) and greater-than (>) operators also work with strings and can be used to determine if a string comes before or after another string in an alphabetical comparison. This can be combined with an equality check by using <= or >=:

```Swift
let string4 = "strung"
```

```Swift
string1 < string2       // returns true
string4 > string2       // returns true
string3 <= string1      // returns true
```

An oft-used check in Objective-C is whether or not a string is empty. This is usually done by comparing to an empty literal string, or by comparing the string's length to 0. Swift provides an isEmpty property to make such hurdles unnecessary, returning true if empty, and false if it contains characters:

```Swift
string1.isEmpty         // returns false
```

Swift's native string comparisons are rounded out with a pair of methods to check if a string contains a given prefix or suffix, again returning true or false if a match was found:

```Swift
string1.hasPrefix("str")    // returns true
string2.hasSuffix("ng")     // returns true
```

Unfortunately, Swift has no native regular expression handling yet, but if you need more complex string matching functionality, you can always take advantage of NSRegularExpression.

MODIFYING STRING CONTENT

While NSString has a mutable counterpart, String does not need one because it can easily be made mutable or immutable by declaring it as a variable or a constant. A string variable can be directly manipulated in a number of ways.

APPENDING A STRING OR CHARACTER

Appending a string to the end of an existing string uses a method named extend:

```Swift
string.extend(".swift")
```

To append a single Character to the end of an existing string, use the append method:

```Swift
let character: Character = "!"
string.append(character)
```

INSERTING A STRING OR CHARACTER

Inserting a string within an existing string requires the `splice` command. This command takes a String to splice and an index for where the splice should take place. This is the same `String.Index` type you used to retrieve individual characters from the string using the subscript operator. As before, you advance the index along to the point where you want to make an insertion, and then pass the new string and the index into the `splice` method:

```swift
var string = "string"
var index = string.startIndex
index = advance(index, 2)
string.splice("utt", atIndex:index)  // becomes "stuttring"
```

If your subconscious tells you that the era of dropping vowels is over, you may want to add a letter. To insert a single character instead of a string, use the `insert` method:

```swift
index = advance(index, 3)
string.insert("e", atIndex:index)     // becomes "stuttering"
```

REPLACING A RANGE OF CHARACTERS

The `replaceRange` method can be used to specify a range of characters to be removed from the existing string and replaced with a new set of characters. The range must be defined in terms of the string's own index.

```swift
var firstIndex = advance(string.startIndex, 1)
var secondIndex = advance(firstIndex, 6)
var range = firstIndex...secondIndex
string.replaceRange(range, with: "imulati")    // becomes "simulating"
```

REMOVING A SINGLE CHARACTER OR A RANGE OF CHARACTERS

To remove a range of characters from an existing string, use the `removeRange` method:

```swift
firstIndex = advance(string.startIndex, 1)
secondIndex = advance(firstIndex, 4)
range = firstIndex...secondIndex
string.removeRange(range)             // becomes "sting"
```

To remove a single character from an existing string, call the `removeAtIndex` method specifying the `String.Index` of the character to remove. This method will also return the removed character:

```swift
firstIndex = advance(string.startIndex, 1)
var removedCharacter = string.removeAtIndex(firstIndex)
println(string)                       // prints "sing"
```

REMOVING ALL CHARACTERS FROM A STRING

To empty a string of its contents, call the removeAll method. It takes a Boolean parameter that indicates whether the existing string's capacity should be retained or not. If you plan on reusing the string, the capacity it already has may be worth keeping as a performance improving measure.

```Swift
string.removeAll(keepCapacity: false)
```

INTERACTING WITH NSSTRING

Although String introduces some useful enhancements over NSString, in some areas NSString still has the edge on its new rival. The good news is that String and NSString are very closely linked—so closely, that they can be used interchangeably throughout your Swift code. You can use String in any API that requires an NSString, and most of the methods available to NSString can be called against a Swift String type. This best-of-both-worlds approach makes life much easier when working with older frameworks, and gives the full range of string handling features to Swift.

To use any of the NSString-specific methods, be sure to import either the Foundation framework directly, or UIKit/AppKit.

SUBSTRINGS

When we looked at creating and examining String objects, one big omission was creating a string from an existing string. This functionality doesn't exist for the Swift String type just yet, but you can use three available methods from NSString instead. When used in Objective-C, these methods take integer indexes, but when used in Swift they take the safer String.Index types.

```Swift
var sourceString = "exponentially"

var fromIndex = advance(sourceString.endIndex, -4)
sourceString.substringFromIndex(fromIndex)

var toIndex = advance(sourceString.startIndex, 8)
sourceString.substringToIndex(toIndex)

fromIndex = advance(sourceString.startIndex, 3)
toIndex = advance(fromIndex, 2)
sourceString.substringWithRange(fromIndex...toIndex)
```

CONVERSIONS

NSString provides a number of helpful string "conversion" methods you've used before. They don't modify the original string but do return a converted version instead.

Swift

```
var conversionString = "swift string"
conversionString = conversionString.uppercaseString
conversionString = conversionString.lowercaseString
conversionString = conversionString.capitalizedString
```

PATH MODIFICATION AND URL METHODS

NSString has a convenient API for working with filesystem paths that has no equivalent in Swift. Take care to note that some of the methods actually return an optional string (String?), so you should handle those appropriately.

Swift

```
var path = "/Users"
path = path.stringByAppendingPathComponent("mkelly")
path = path.stringByAppendingPathComponent("Documents")
path = path.stringByAppendingPathComponent("Swift Translation Guide")
path = path.stringByAppendingPathComponent("Strings")
path = path.stringByAppendingPathExtension("swift")!

path = path.stringByDeletingPathExtension
path = path.stringByDeletingLastPathComponent
```

It can also handle some URL encoding issues on your behalf:

Swift

```
path = path.stringByAddingPercentEscapesUsingEncoding(NSASCIIStringEncoding)!
```

EXPLICITLY CREATING AN NSSTRING

Although the string types can be freely interchanged, creating an explicit NSString or NSMutableString from Swift code is still possible:

Swift

```
var nsString = NSString(format: "From %@", "NSString")
let nsMutableString = NSMutableString(format: "From %@", "NSString")
nsMutableString.replaceCharactersInRange(NSRange(location: 5, length: 8),
→ withString: "NSMutableString")
```

Note that an NSString object can be assigned to a Swift variable, but that *doesn't* make it mutable—instead the variable nsString can be pointed to another NSString object.

Also note that you created an NSMutableString and assigned it to a constant, yet were able to modify its contents. Again, it's only the reference that is constant and cannot be altered.

Because these behaviors are counterintuitive, stick with Swift types where possible. If your existing code makes heavy use of NSString (especially methods that might not be available to Swift strings, such as length), you may wish to use explicit NSString references while porting existing code to Swift.

UNICODE

Swift strings are fully Unicode aware, so some tradeoffs have to be made to handle them safely. We've already seen that indexes on strings have to be handled by advancing a special index value forward or backward in the string. This may seem like an excessive level of abstraction, but consider the following Irish name:

```Swift
var accentedString = "Aoibhínn"
```

This name contains an accented character, which is often overlooked because it replaces the dot on the letter "i". If you were to count the *characters*, here it would return 8.

```Swift
countElements(accentedString)          // returns 8
```

However, if you were to count the *Unicode* bytes, it will instead be 9. You can do this by asking the string for its utf8 view, and counting the elements of it:

```Swift
countElements(accentedString.utf8)     // returns 9
```

In this case, the accented letter is represented as two bytes, which is an example of why you need to use advance to move through the string rather than using a basic letter-counting technique.

> **NOTE:** String also has representations in UTF16, utf16, and as unicode scalars, unicodeScalars.

Swift's string comparison operators are smart enough to take into account the differences between UTF encodings. For example, the name "Aoibhínn" can be typed in directly, or can be constructed by combining the "i" and an acute accent character:

```Swift
var alternativeConstruction = "Aoibhi\u{301}nn"
```

Counting the elements of the alternative construction still yields 8 characters, though the UTF8 representation will vary from that of unicodeString.utf8:

```Swift
countElements(alternativeConstruction)          // returns 8
countElements(alternativeConstruction.utf8)     // returns 10
```

When comparing strings, Swift takes Unicode characters into account. Even though they were constructed differently, and have different byte counts, performing a direct comparison on these two strings will still produce a match.

```
accentedString == alternativeConstruction   // returns true
```

WRAPPING UP

Compared to Objective-C, Swift feels like a more modern language, simply by virtue of having a native string implementation. Although it doesn't fully match up to `NSString` in terms of API and convenience methods, features like full Unicode support make it very powerful, especially as app development begins to embrace localizations. Virtually transparent bridging between `String` and `NSString` means that the best-of-both-worlds is available to developers who want to wrangle as much from their strings as possible.

The next chapter looks at Swift's implementation of classes.

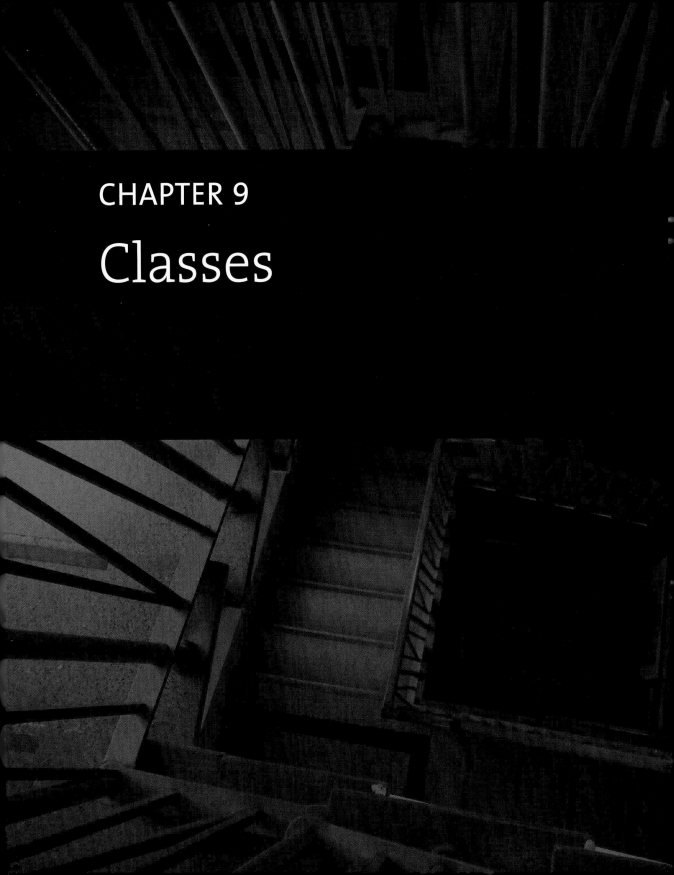

CHAPTER 9
Classes

Swift is an object-oriented programming (OOP) language, just like Objective-C. The defining principles of OOP are inheritance, polymorphism, and encapsulation, and all these principles are implemented in Swift by the class.

CREATING CLASSES

To define a class in Objective-C required two files (one for the header and one for the implementation) and special keywords in the files to indicate where the `@interface` and `@implementation` sections should go.

Swift simplifies the definition of a class by requiring the keyword `class`, followed by the class name and a set of curly braces, and only has to be created in one file:

Swift

```swift
class VolumeControl {

}
```

That is all it takes to create a class. You can instantiate it by calling the empty initializer:

Swift

```swift
let volumeControl = VolumeControl()
```

Unfortunately, you can't do a whole lot with this class right now because it has no methods or data.

METHODS

In Chapter 6, we examined Swift functions and highlighted that a method is just a function attached to an object type. This means the syntax for defining a method is exactly the same as that for a function, the major difference being the method is defined within the `class` block. Methods in Swift are declared inline:

Swift

```swift
class VolumeControl {
    func pumpItUp() { }
}
```

To execute the method, you use the member access operator (`.`) on an instance value, and then call it like you would a function:

Swift

```swift
volumeControl.pumpItUp()
```

Unlike global functions, object methods can be class methods (known as *type methods* in Swift terminology) or instance methods. In Objective-C, we differentiate between class and instance methods by prefixing their prototype (or declaration) with a plus (+) or minus (-) sign. In Swift, all methods are deemed to be instance methods unless they are declared with the `class` keyword before the `func` keyword:

Swift

```swift
class VolumeControl {
    func pumpItUp() { }
    class func controlName() -> String { return "Volume" }
}
```

As with Objective-C, you must call type methods on the class type and not an instance value:

```Swift
VolumeControl.controlName()
```

In Objective-C, developers commonly use the `class` property of an instance value to obtain the class type, and use that to call class methods. This can by done in Swift using the `dynamicType` property available to class instances:

```Swift
volumeControl.dynamicType.controlName()
```

PROPERTIES

Properties in Objective-C are defined using the following syntax:

```Objective-C
@property type name;
```

This performs some background tasks to create an instance variable (or *ivar*) to represent the property, to create a getter method so the property value can be accessed, and to create a setter method so the property value can be updated. No mean feat for a short line of code.

Properties in Swift are significantly different and come in two distinct flavors: stored properties and computed properties.

STORED PROPERTIES

A stored property in Swift is analogous to a regular property in Objective-C. They are declared as a constant or variable inside the `class` body:

```Swift
class VolumeControl {
    var level = 0
    let maxLevel = 9
}
```

In this example is a property named `level` initialized with a value of 0. Stored properties must be assigned an initial value before use, either at the point of declaration or in an initializer. We don't have an initializer yet, so this code assigns a value to `level` here. As with regular variables and constants, properties can take advantage of type inference—here it is inferred to be an `Int`—and they can also be optional types.

To read the property value, use the member access operator (`.`) on the class instance followed by the property name:

```Swift
var level: Int
level = volumeControl.level      // returns 0
level = volumeControl.maxLevel   // returns 9
```

To set a new value, use the member access operator on the class instance followed by the property name and an assignment operator. Note that constant properties cannot be updated in this way.

Swift

```
volumeControl.level = 1
level = volumeControl.level      //  returns 1
volumeControl.maxLevel = 5       //  causes an error
```

This is similar to Objective-C's dot syntax, but with a crucial difference. In Objective-C, dot syntax is an alternative way to call underlying methods with a predefined naming scheme. This could also be expressed as:

Objective-C

```
NSInteger level;
level = [volumeControl level];
[volumeControl setLevel:1];
level = [volumeControl level];
```

Swift has no such equivalent; defining a stored property named level does not automatically create a pair of methods named setLevel(Int) and level() -> Int.

This has another implication for Objective-C developers—not having the ability to implement these methods for a stored property means a number of patterns commonly employed through setters and getters are not possible:

- Using the setter to calculate and update another property
- Determining if the property *should* be updated
- Calling other methods in response to the property changing
- Lazily initializing a property

Fortunately, Swift has a number of new features you can use to achieve the same effects: computed properties, lazy stored properties, and property observers.

COMPUTED PROPERTIES

A *computed property* has no underlying variable to be modified and is used as a means to manipulate other properties. You can define a computed property by specifying a getter method and an optional setter method after the property definition:

Swift

```
var internalLevel = 0
var level: Int {
    get {
        return internalLevel
    }
    set(newLevel) {
        internalLevel = newLevel
    }
}
```

A computed property is indicated by the presence of a code block after the variable or constant definition. Within the block, the get and set methods should be specified. Unlike for a regular method or function definition, the get method does not include parentheses or a return type, which is inferred from the property type.

The set method can be defined with no parameter type required, or a shorthand form can be adopted that drops the parameter name completely. When this shorthand form is used, the supplied parameter is assumed to be named newValue:

```Swift
var internalLevel = 0
var level: Int {
    get {
        return internalLevel
    }
    set {
        internalLevel = newValue
    }
}
```

If a setter is not required, it should be omitted:

```Swift
var internalLevel = 0
var level: Int {
    get {
        return internalLevel
    }
}
```

As another optimization, a computed property with only a getter can be condensed down further to:

```Swift
var internalLevel = 0
var level: Int {
    return internalLevel
}
```

Computed properties can also be defined at the type level using the keyword class, where they are known as *type properties*. Stored properties cannot be defined as type properties, and this means that computed type properties are limited to computing values from their own data, from other type properties, or from type methods.

LAZY STORED PROPERTIES

Although you can use computed properties to perform lazy initialization, this is such a common pattern in Objective-C code that the Swift developers have introduced a lazy keyword to apply to stored properties.

The pattern most often used in Objective-C involves checking the value of the property on each access. If the property is not `nil`, it is generally returned immediately; if it is `nil`, it is calculated or set up, stored for next time, and returned. For example:

Objective-C

```objc
- (UIView *)volumeView {
    if (_volumeView == nil) {
        _volumeView = [[UIView alloc] init];
    }
    return _volumeView;
}
```

This is a useful pattern and has worked well for many years, but needs a lot of unnecessary extra code written every time lazy initialization is required. To replicate this in Swift requires making the property an optional type, putting additional overhead on calling code to handle an option.

With lazy stored properties, this boilerplate code is mostly removed:

Swift

```swift
lazy var volumeView = UIView()
```

Until the property is directly accessed, the potentially time-consuming view initialization code does not need to be executed.

PROPERTY OBSERVERS

Property observers are a pair of methods (which must be called `willSet` and `didSet`) that can optionally be set up on any stored property. They are executed before and after the property is updated. This gives you the facility to react to the new value, and potentially change it.

Property observers can be used to replicate some of the abilities of key-value observing (KVO) in Objective-C, which has no direct equivalent in Swift. The property observers could be set up to perform callbacks to observing classes in the event of a property change.

To set up property observers, define the property as normal, and add a block afterwards containing a method definition for `willSet`, `didSet`, or both:

Swift

```swift
var internalLevel: Int = 0 {
    willSet(newInternalLevel) {
        if newInternalLevel > maxLevel {
            println("Level \(newInternalLevel) will exceed max. Preventing this.")
        }
    }
    didSet(oldInternalLevel) {
        if oldInternalLevel == maxLevel {
            internalLevel = maxLevel
        }
    }
}
```

In the `willSet` method, the passed parameter (which has the same type as the property itself) contains the new value of the property to which it is going to be updated. This gives you an opportunity to perform actions in anticipation of the update (for example, saving the old value, or logging the action), but does not give you the ability to change it. The name of the parameter being passed, and the parentheses, can be omitted, in which case a default parameter name of `newValue` can be assumed inside the method body:

```swift
willSet {
    if newValue > maxLevel {
        println("Level \(newValue) will exceed max. Preventing this.")
    }
}
```

Swift

Similarly, the `didSet` method has a passed parameter (again with the same type as the property) that contains the old value of the property from which it has just been updated. As well as being able to perform actions in response to the change, you can also update the property value itself. This could be used as part of a validation process—if the new value was not within a valid range it could be reset back to the old value or to a safe default. Like the `willSet` method, the passed parameter can be omitted from the declaration and a default parameter name of `oldValue` can be assumed inside the method body:

```swift
didSet {
    if oldValue == maxLevel {
        internalLevel = maxLevel
    }
}
```

Swift

READ-ONLY PROPERTIES

In Objective-C, we are able to mark a property as read-only by adding the `readonly` modifier to the `@property` definition. Marking an Objective-C property as read-only does not perform any special action on the ivar, it just results in no setter method being created to allow changes to the ivar from outside the instance.

Unfortunately, Swift does not have a direct equivalent to the `readonly` modifier. Creating the property using a constant will not suffice because the constant can be set only once; it certainly makes the property read-only to calling code, but it also makes the property read-only from inside the class instance as well.

To achieve this with Swift requires using two properties: a private internal property and a public computed property that has only a getter. To make a property private, it needs to be marked with the `private` keyword (discussed later in the section "Access Control"). We can change the class to achieve this as follows:

Swift

```swift
class VolumeControl {
    private var internalLevel: Int = 0 { ... }
    var level: Int {
        return internalLevel
    }
}
```

Although this might seem a clunky solution, it isn't much different from how Objective-C actually handles it.

THINK ABOUT YOUR SELF

So far we have yet to encounter a call from one method to another method in the same instance of a class, or an access of a property from within an instance method. If you're thinking like an Objective-C developer, you might suggest using self but in more of a Swift way like self.method() or self.property.

This is valid in Swift but not always necessary. For most of your internal access needs, you can get away without using self, but when a method or initializer has a parameter that has the same name as a property, you should use self to remove any ambiguity.

INITIALIZERS

Creating an instance of a class in Swift is different from Objective-C, where you first have to call the alloc class method to create an instance, and then call one of the initializer methods to set up the fresh instance. Swift retains the concept of initializer methods in name, but they behave more like constructors in C++ or Java.

When you define a new class, it comes with a default initializer named init. This initializer takes no parameters and can be used to create an instance of the class:

Swift

```swift
let volumeControl = VolumeControl.init()
```

The Swift developers are obviously conscious of how often developers have to type the alloc/init combination in Objective-C, and have removed the need to actually type init in Swift. As a result, this shortened form will work also (and is preferable):

Swift

```swift
let volumeControl = VolumeControl()
```

NOTE: This default initializer is created automatically only because all the stored properties have initial values assigned. If this weren't the case, or you wanted to perform additional customization, you would need to create one or more of your own initializers.

CREATING INITIALIZERS

Creating custom initializers is something we all had to do in Objective-C, and there is no reason to suspect that Swift will be any different. In Swift, initializers differ from regular methods in that they are not prefixed with the `func` keyword, and are always named `init`:

```
init() { }
```

Unlike an Objective-C initializer method, the Swift `init` does not return anything. All it needs to do is set up the instance ready for use, usually by assigning initial values to any stored properties not already assigned a value at declaration time, or that should be updated with new values passed to custom initializers.

All initializers in Swift must be named `init`, so the only way to differentiate between them is through parameter types and parameter names. Consider the `UIView` class—it has three initializers:

- `init()`
- `init(coder: NSCoder)`
- `init(frame: CGRect)`

When creating initializers, ensure that all stored properties have been assigned initial values before the initializer returns, or before performing any calls to `self` (implicit or otherwise). The exception to this is when dealing with a *convenience*, or delegating, initializer.

USING CONVENIENCE AND DESIGNATED INITIALIZERS

The concept of designated and convenience initializers exists in Objective-C but in a less formal capacity. An initializer is deemed to be a designated initializer if it is responsible for invoking the designated initializer of its superclass. A convenience, or secondary, initializer is expected to defer to the designated initializer for initial setup after which it can get on with the process of customizing the setup.

Swift introduces a new keyword, `convenience`, that can be applied to an `init` method to indicate it is a convenience method and must delegate initial setup responsibilities to a designated initializer (indicated by the absence of the `convenience` keyword).

As well as being marked with the keyword, a convenience initializer must make a call to a designated initializer *in the same class*, and it must make that call before setting values for any stored properties. This ensures the instance is fully set up before any other customization is performed.

Consider the example `VolumeControl` class. It currently has a single initializer but has no need to set any values. The control has two stored properties, `maxLevel` and `internalLevel`, and being able to set these values at startup would be useful. To do so, you create a designated initializer with the ability to set these values:

Swift

```swift
class VolumeControl {
    init(maxLevel: Int, initialLevel: Int) {
        self.maxLevel = maxLevel
        self.internalLevel = initialLevel
    }

    let maxLevel: Int = 10
    private var internalLevel: Int = 0
    var level: Int {
        return internalLevel
    }
}
```

You can now instantiate a class with a restricted maximum volume level (maybe for the people with sensitive hearing) using custom settings like this:

Swift

```swift
var restrictedVolumeControl = VolumeControl(maxLevel: 7, initialLevel: 3)
```

Any previous instances created using the plain VolumeControl() form are now invalid. By defining a designated initializer, you need to use it or provide alternatives in the form of convenience initializer. To make the old instances work again, you can create a convenience initializer that takes no arguments:

Swift

```swift
convenience init() {
    self.init(maxLevel: 10, initialLevel: 7)
}
```

You can also create further convenience initializers with other combinations of values:

Swift

```swift
convenience init(goesToEleven: Bool) {
    if goesToEleven {
        self.init(maxLevel: 11, initialLevel: 11)
    } else {
        self.init()
    }
}
```

This provides the opportunity to create a "proper" volume control:

Swift

```swift
var tufnelVolumeControl = VolumeControl(goesToEleven: true)
```

DEINITIALIZING

Like Objective-C, Swift object lifecycles are managed by automatic reference counting, and are destroyed when the last reference to the object is removed. Swift provides a hook for you to perform your own cleanup actions just before the object is fully destroyed. If you have resources to clean up, you can put suitable code into a method named deinit. Like dealloc in Objective-C, you should never call this method directly. If you are expecting this method to be called and it's not happening, you may have a memory management problem. Memory management in Swift is based on automatic reference counting (ARC), so much of your understanding from Objective-C is still valid in Swift. See the Appendix for some more information.

INHERITANCE

Although structures and enumerations are also object types in Swift, only the class object type can inherit data and functionality from other classes. If you started with a structure and found you needed a parent object of some type, you may need to switch to using a class object type instead.

Inheritance in Objective-C and Swift has one significant difference: An object in Swift does not need to inherit from a base class, whereas in Objective-C, all objects must inherit from a base class like NSObject (or from another class that has inherited from a base class).

> **NOTE:** If you are working with Objective-C code (detailed in Chapter 14), you need to make your Swift class inherit from a base class—in most cases NSObject **will do.**

If you want to introduce a class hierarchy to your Swift code, you can make a class inherit from another class at the point of declaration by typing a colon (:) after the class name, and specifying the name of the superclass from which it should inherit. In the VolumeControl class, you may want to create and inherit from a more basic control. To do so, you must define the superclass, then implement the inheritance:

```
class BasicControl {


}
```

Swift

```
class VolumeControl : BasicControl {
    //  Rest of existing VolumeControl class
}
```

OVERRIDING A METHOD

If you've been following along with the code examples, you will receive an error in your playground using the previous code because of a conflict between the init methods in Basic-Control and VolumeControl. Unlike in Objective-C, overriding a method from a superclass isn't possible without explicitly saying that you intend to do so.

The reason for this is once again safety: By making the developer explicitly state the override is intentional, a user is less likely to inadvertently "highjack" methods from a superclass without realizing. You can state your intention by using the override keyword in front of the method declaration. In the VolumeControl class, add the override keyword as follows:

Swift

```
class VolumeControl : BasicControl {
    convenience override init() {
        self.init(maxLevel: 10, initialLevel: 7)
    }
    //  Rest of existing VolumeControl class
}
```

You need to use the override keyword when re-declaring any entity in a subclass that already exists in the superclass.

CALLING TO THE SUPERCLASS

Now that you have a superclass, the designated initializer should be updated to call the designated initializer of the superclass. Every instance of a class that inherits from a superclass has an implicit property named super that acts as a reference to the superclass. Our designated initializer can be updated like this:

Swift

```
init(maxLevel: Int, initialLevel: Int) {
    self.maxLevel = maxLevel
    self.internalLevel = initialLevel
    super.init()
}
```

Another key difference exists between Swift and Objective-C: In Objective-C, the call to the superclass must be performed first to ensure that the object is fully created before it is used. In Swift, the opposite is true: You must always ensure that all the initialization is completed in the subclass before calling up to the superclass. This is applicable only at initialization time, and you may call up to the superclass at any point within your regular methods.

ACCESS CONTROL

Unlike many other OOP languages, Objective-C doesn't really have a proper system for controlling access to private data and methods. You can give the illusion of privacy, but in practice it can be circumvented—this is why an app can be rejected for using private APIs.

In the name of modernization, the Swift developers have introduced a system of real access controls to the language. Swift has three levels of access: private, internal, and public. All three can apply to just about any entity in Swift.

PRIVATE

A private entity, as marked with the `private` modifier keyword, cannot be accessed outside its current "container." When applied to a property or method in a class or structure, a private entity cannot be accessed by code outside the file in which the class is defined. This is similar to the effect you achieve using the class extension category in Objective-C. By creating a property that is declared only in the class extension in the implementation file, the property can be effectively hidden from other code, which has visibility of only the header file:

Objective-C

```
@interface VolumeControl        //  File: VolumeControl.h
@end


#import "VolumeControl.h"       //  File: VolumeControl.m


@interface VolumeControl ()
@property (readwrite, assign) NSInteger level;
@end
```

Replicating the read-only public property for `level` which you set up in the section "Read-Only Properties," requires adding a readonly property to the header file:

Objective-C

```
@interface VolumeControl        //  File: VolumeControl.h
@property (readonly, assign) NSInteger level;
@end


#import "VolumeControl.h"       //  File: VolumeControl.m


@interface VolumeControl ()
@property (readwrite, assign) NSInteger level;
@end
```

The equivalent in Swift is considerably more compact and maintainable:

Swift

```
private var internalLevel: Int = 0
```

More importantly, it's truly read-only. On the other hand, using key-value coding in Objective-C is all you need to update the publicly read-only property:

Objective-C

```
VolumeControl *volumeControl = [[VolumeControl alloc] init];
[volumeControl setValue:@(3) forKey:@"level"];
```

When applied to an entity such as a global variable or an object type definition, the `private` keyword prevents visibility of the entity outside the containing file. If you have an entity that is relevant only to a specific file (a string, or an enumeration for example), you may wish to make them private so they are not exposed to the rest of the project.

INTERNAL

The default level of access for any constant, variable, function, or method is internal. While you can explicitly state that a value is internal using the `internal` keyword, using no access modifier keywords implies the same.

When you define an entity as being internally visible, you are saying that you wish it to be accessible to the code in the same *module*. In Swift, a module is equivalent to the Xcode target in which the code resides—this could be an app target, a framework, or a test target.

While the potential uses for this are limited regarding app targets, it will be very useful when developing frameworks, because it allows developers to choose exactly what is exposed to consumers of their framework. Marking a class as internal makes it available for use by the remainder of your target, but restricted from the rest of the world.

PUBLIC

When an entity is marked as public, using the `public` keyword, the entity is available for use just about anywhere you care to imagine. Use this level of accessibility only for data and code where you are confident that it's safe to be exposed to the world at large.

SUBSCRIPTING

The subscript operator allows types such as classes, structures, and enumerations to provide random access to their contents in a similar way to arrays and dictionaries. Objective-C introduced the ability to add subscript notation to a class through the adoption of one of two pairs of methods.

For array-style subscripting, the class needs to implement the `-objectAtIndexedSubscript:` method to retrieve a value at a given index, and the `-setObject:atIndexedSubscript:` method to assign a value to a given index. For dictionary-style subscripting, the class needs to implement the `-objectForKeyedSubscript:` method to retrieve a value for a given key, and the `-setObject:forKeyedSubscript:` method to assign a value for a given key.

To achieve the same behavior in Swift requires the implementation of subscript functions. To do so, use `subscript` inside your object type definition, indicate the types that are received by the subscript operator as an index, indicate the type that should be returned, and then implement a pair of methods named get and set. The get method should determine a value to return based on the index types. The `set` method receives a new value of the specified type and should store or process the value based on those types.

Swift

```
subscript(IndexTypes) -> ValueType {
    get { ... }
    set(newValue) { ... }
}
```

The subscript operators in Swift far exceed the capabilities of those in Objective-C. Defining an index type of an Int in Swift reproduces the behavior of a standard array, while other index types act more like a dictionary. You can even supply multiple types to use as the index should the need arise. The get method is essential for a subscript to operate, but the set method can be omitted to produce a read-only subscript. In this example, you implement a way to return the actual level for some named volume levels:

Swift

```swift
subscript(levelName: String) -> Int? {
    get {
        switch levelName {
            case "Off":
                return 0
            case "Min":
                return 1
            case "Mid":
                return (maxLevel / 2)
            case "Max":
                return maxLevel
            default:
                return nil
        }
    }
}
```

Subscripts are not limited to just one per type—you can have as many subscript definitions as you can think of different type signatures. Just don't go overboard; subscripts are a very useful feature, but you shouldn't abuse them just to take advantage of them—using subscripts in a non-obvious way can make your code much harder to read and maintain.

WRAPPING UP

Classes have been made more powerful in Swift, yet remain easier and safer than ever to use through a more compact and simplified syntax. The addition of keywords like lazy, subscript, and convenience have codified existing patterns in Objective-C into full features of Swift classes. Fortunately classes have received such attention, because they now have some serious competition.

The next chapter looks at the enhancements Swift brings to structures and enumerations that show how they've become a serious alternative to the use of classes.

CHAPTER 10

Structures and Enumerations

Look out classes, you're no longer the only object type in town. Swift has given both structures and enumerations the power to associate functions with the data they act upon. This transforms structures and enumerations from being simple data types, to being complex object types, causing the lines dividing them to become increasingly blurred. This chapter picks up where the last chapter on classes left off and aims to help distinguish between the three types. By explaining the subtle differences between them, we hope to make it easier to decide precisely which type you need.

STRUCTURES

In the hierarchy of the three object types in Swift, structures are most certainly in the middle with respect to capability. Structures are capable of much of the complexity of classes, yet are not able to inherit from a "super struct," making them less useful from an OOP perspective. Despite this, they're still a very capable data type, and for storing small data quantities with some associated methods, they are an extremely useful tool.

DEFINING A STRUCTURE

To create a structure, you use the `struct` keyword followed by a block delineated with curly braces. To store data in the structure, define properties just as you would for a class. In this example, you're going to use a structure to model the pertinent properties of a Spinal Tap album cover:

Swift

```
struct AlbumCover {
    var blackLevel: Float = 0.0
    var sexistPicture: Bool = false
}
```

To create an instance of a structure type, call it by its initializer:

Swift

```
var albumCover = AlbumCover()
```

All structures come with a default *memberwise initializer*. Despite not defining an explicit initializer, the example structure comes with a default one that allows you to specify a value for `blackLevel` and `sexistPicture` directly:

Swift

```
let almostBlackCover = AlbumCover(blackLevel: 0.9, sexistPicture: false)
```

> **NOTE:** These kind of initializers are especially useful for defining constants—the entire structure can be initialized and created as a single operation.
> Using an empty initializer will often require assignment to a variable so that the data can be adjusted; this opens the variable to subsequent, and possibly undesired, modification.

Like classes, structure properties must always be initialized through initial value assignment or by an initializer.

They can also have type methods and properties; though, unlike in classes, these are not indicated through the `class` keyword. When defining type methods, you should use the `static` keyword before the `func` keyword; for type properties use the `static` keyword before the `var` or `let` keywords:

```
struct AlbumCover {
    static func couldBeBlacker(blackLevel: Float) -> Bool {
        return blackLevel != blackestLevel
    }
    static let blackestLevel: Float = 1.0
}
```

NOTE: Structures can also have stored properties as type properties, whereas classes are limited to computed type properties only.

STRUCTURES AND C STRUCTS

You may think you haven't spent much time working with C structs before, but most iOS and OS X developers have spent plenty of time dealing with CGRects, which is definitely a struct type. A struct in C is a pure representation of data, and unlike a Swift structure, has no associated methods for acting upon the data.

This is very evident when dealing with structs like CGRect and its companions from the CoreGraphics framework. A CGRect in Objective-C has no equivalent to a structure initializer; you can either create the struct the old-school way by directly populating the data members, or by using a convenience function that takes the relevant parameters and spits out a populated CGRect on the other end.

```
CGRect rect = { { 50, 50 } , { 100, 100} };
// or
rect = CGRectMake(50, 50, 100, 100);
// or if you like C99 style:
rect = (CGRect){ .origin = { .x = 50, .y = 50 }, .size = { .width = 100,
→ .height = 100 } };
```

None of these methods is particularly user friendly (although some developers—you know who you are—do have a penchant for C99 style), particularly for ordering large numbers of parameters. The convenience functions have also grown to be a large collection of useful functions, but they're harder to remember and search through. For example, to get the height property from a CGRect you can use either of these techniques:

```
CGFloat height = rect.size.height;
// or
height = CGRectGetHeight(rect);
```

The first technique requires knowledge of the internal layout of the struct, and the second requires an indirect function, to which the struct is passed, to be queried—neither is particularly intuitive.

Swift structures have initializers to create their data, and methods that can act directly on that data. When used in Swift, a CGRect can be created as follows:

```
let rect = CGRect(x:50, y:50, width:100, height:100)
```

The height of the rect is exposed as a property and can be accessed directly from the structure using:

```
let height = rect.height
```

STRUCTURES AND SWIFT CLASSES

Structures can have initializers, methods, and properties, which raises the obvious question: Why use classes when structures can do so much? This very valid question is one of a series of questions every Swift developer should ask when realizing a need to model some data in an app. Some very important differences between classes and structures affect the choice.

A key difference is that structures do not support inheritance. If your data model requires your data entity be extended, or that it should extend another entity, then the data should be created as a class. Note, however, that both structures and classes support implementing protocols and both can be extended; we delve further into both these topics in Chapter 13.

Unlike classes, structures cannot be passed by reference. When you pass a structure as a parameter to, or as a return value from, a function, it is copied. Any changes you make to the structure while in a function do not affect the original structure. If you need to pass data entities around, you need to use classes.

Because structures are copied, rather than passed by reference, their internal data will need to be copied as well. A structure that contains large quantities of data can affect the performance of your applications through wasted CPU cycles and excess memory usage. If your data entity stores large quantities of data, consider classes instead of structures.

Structures do not have a deinit method for cleaning them up when they are disposed of. If you need the ability to clean up resources when your data entity goes out of scope, consider using a class instead.

MODIFYING A STRUCTURE

Making changes to the data in a structure follows slightly different rules than the modification of classes, because of the different ways the two types are handled.

The most direct way to modify a structure is to change data through an exposed variable property. In the example structure, you can change the value of the blackLevel property using dot syntax:

```
albumCover.blackLevel = 0.5
```

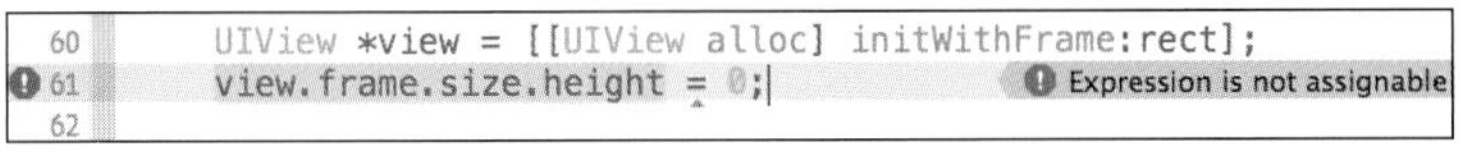

FIGURE 10.1 Objective-C does not allow direct modification of a view's frame.

In Swift you can directly modify a "property of a property," which removes one of the more frustrating limitations of Objective-C. If you have ever had to change properties of the frame in a UIView, you know that, in Objective-C, you can't directly modify a value such as the frame height without composing a new frame structure (**Figure 10.1**).

The workaround for this has always been to take a copy of the frame and create a new frame based on the existing frame properties, substituting those you wish to change. Now in Swift, you can directly modify the individual properties of the frame:

```
var view = UIView(frame: rect)
view.frame.size.height = 0
```

Swift

If you want to define a method on your structure that modifies its contents, that method must be marked with the keyword mutating. Consider the following method that sets the blackLevel property to be as black as it can be:

```
struct AlbumCover {
    var blackLevel: Float = 0.0
    var sexistPicture: Bool = false
    mutating func makeNoneBlacker() {
        blackLevel = 1.0
    }
}
```

Swift

Try removing the mutating keyword; Xcode will raise an error indicating that you cannot modify blackLevel.

Like classes, structures support computed properties, which can also use a setter to modify the internal data. Strangely, a setter for a computed property is capable of changing the internal data even without a mutating keyword.

Unlike a class, a constant reference to a structure is truly immutable. Whether you try to modify a property directly, through a computed property, or using a mutating function, if the structure reference is a constant you will receive a compiler error. This is in direct contrast to a class, for which only the reference is immutable, but the internal data can still be modified.

Because structures are treated as values, their behavior is also affected when they are assigned to multiple variables or constants. A structure can have only one reference, whereas a class can have multiple references. If you try to assign a structure to another reference, you get a copy instead. You can see this illustrated in the following example:

```
var smellTheGlove = AlbumCover()
var theWhiteAlbum = smellTheGlove
smellTheGlove.blackLevel = 1.0
smellTheGlove.blackLevel            // returns 1.0
theWhiteAlbum.blackLevel            // returns 0.0
```

Swift

ENUMERATIONS

Despite their simplicity in the world of C, enumerations (enums) have long been an essential part of OS X and iOS development. Enums permeate the Apple frameworks and are used for defining error codes, options, and behaviors. The benefit in the existing enum type is that plain old integers can be represented as more meaningful values. Although you would eventually learn that –[UITableViewCell cellAccessory] having a value of 0 means no accessory and 1 means a disclosure indicator, it is certainly a lot easier to remember UITableViewCellAccessoryNone and UITableViewCellAccessoryDisclosureIndicator. The downside is that enums just use integers to represent their data, and it's perfectly possible to compare one "type" of enum to another resulting in subtle coding errors.

Swift not only gives enumerations their full title, but also bestows upon them some extra capabilities. Enumerations can use more than just integers as their underlying raw data type; they can have computed properties and can have methods that operate on their data.

CREATING ENUMERATIONS

Creating an enumeration in Swift is also a straightforward process, compared to the typedef dance required in Objective-C. An enumeration is defined using the enum keyword, followed by the enumeration name and a block in which the cases can be defined. Here you define a VolumeLevel enumeration to go with the VolumeControl class in Chapter 9:

Swift

```
enum VolumeLevel {
    case Off
    case Min
    case Mid
    case Max
}
```

The case statements define the individual items of data the enumeration represents and can appear on individual lines or be placed on a single line separated by commas:

Swift

```
enum VolumeLevel {
    case Off, Min, Mid, Max
}
```

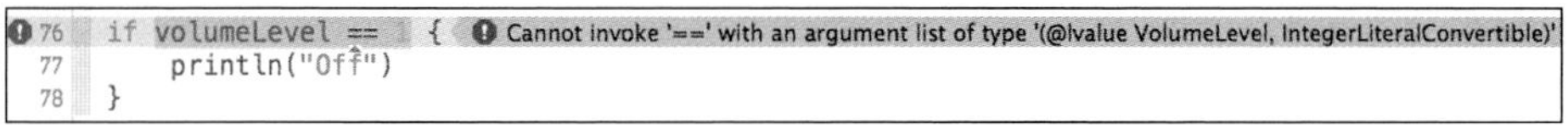

FIGURE 10.2
An enumeration can be compared only to a value of the same type.

USING ENUMERATIONS

To use an enumeration, you can use it directly or assign it to a variable or constant:

```swift
var volumeLevel = VolumeLevel.Off
```

A case can be used directly as part of a conditional operation:

```swift
if volumeLevel == VolumeLevel.Off {
    println("Off")
}
```

What you can't do is compare a VolumeLevel value to any other type; VolumeLevel is a type, which means that it can be compared only to another VolumeLevel. Even trying to compare to a number, as you could easily do in Objective-C, will not suffice (**Figure 10.2**).

SHORTENED NAME SYNTAX

If you have ever tired of typing (or even just tabbing through an autocompletion list for) enums like UITableViewCellAccessoryDisclosureIndicator, you'll be very pleased that you can access Swift enumerations using just the case name in situations where it can infer the type. For example, you could reassign the variable volumeLevel and test against it like this:

```swift
volumeLevel = .Max
```

```swift
if volumeLevel == .Max {
    println("Max")
}
```

This is an exceptionally useful feature, especially when functions and methods use enumerations to define their parameters and return values. It can also save a lot of typing on switch statements:

```swift
switch volumeLevel {
case .Off:
    println("Off")
case .Min:
    println("Min")
case .Mid:
    println("Mid")
case .Max:
    println("Max")
}
```

WORKING WITH RAW VALUES

Unlike the "always integer" enums in C, enumerations in Swift have no underlying type by default. You can change this by specifying a type on the initial line of the declaration. To use a classic integer-based enumeration starting at 0, you do something like this:

Swift

```
enum VolumeLevel: Int {
    case Off, Min, Mid, Max
}
```

Like C enums, you can specify values for individual cases, just a starting point, or a combination:

Swift

```
enum VolumeLevel: Int {
    case Off = 0, Min, Mid = 5, Max = 10
}
```

Any type can be used for the raw value, but if it isn't an integer type, you need to specify a value for each case:

Swift

```
enum VolumeLevel: String {
    case Off = "Off", Min = "Minimum", Mid = "Mid-level", Max = "Maximum"
}
```

To get at this underlying data, you can use the `rawValue` property on an enumeration case or an enumeration instance:

Swift

```
VolumeLevel.Mid.rawValue     //  Returns "Mid-level"
```

Using raw values to store information like human-readable strings can reduce the need for `switch` statements like the one you used earlier. Instead of switching on `volumeLevel`, then checking each case, simply calling `println(volumeLevel.rawValue)` replaces the entire `switch` statement.

Raw values can also be used to create a new enumeration instance by passing a raw value to an initializer:

Swift

```
var maximumLevel = VolumeLevel(rawValue: "Maximum")
```

Passing a bad value to this initializer would be very easy so the return type is actually an optional `VolumeLevel`. It will have a value if a valid raw value was passed, or will be `nil` otherwise.

ASSOCIATED VALUES

Raw value types are an extremely useful addition to enumerations, but that's not all that can be achieved. Swift allows for the association of arbitrary data types with the individual cases of an enumeration. If you felt limited because raw values all had to be the same type, this may be the feature for you. Note that you cannot combine raw values and associated values.

To use an associated value with a case, you first need to specify the data types the case can accept:

```
enum VolumeLevel {
    case Off
    case Min(Int)
    case Mid(minLevel: Int, maxLevel: Int)
    case Max(Int)
    case Tufnel(String)
}
```

The means that constructing each volume level case now varies: Creating the .Off case requires no parameters, creating .Min and .Max requires an Int value, and creating the .Mid case requires two *named* parameters. The last case varies even more and simply takes a string. To construct each of these, you do this:

```
var currentLevel: VolumeLevel
currentLevel = .Off;
currentLevel = .Min(1)
currentLevel = .Mid(minLevel: 1, maxLevel: 10)
currentLevel = .Max(10)
currentLevel = .Tufnel("It's one louder")
```

To take advantage of the values associated, you can assign them to variables or constants during a switch statement to extract them:

```
switch currentLevel {
    case .Off:
        println("Off is always 0")
    case .Min(let minLevel):
        println("Minimim level: \(minLevel)")
    case .Mid(let minLevel, let maxLevel):
        let midLevel = (maxLevel - minLevel) / 2
        println("Medium level: \(midLevel)")
    case .Max(let level):
        println("Maximum level: \(level)")
    case .Tufnel(let nigelSpeaks):
        print("Nigel says: \(nigelSpeaks)");
}
```

METHODS AND COMPUTED PROPERTIES

Like structures, enumerations in Swift can have their own methods and computed properties. Common patterns in Objective-C, like providing a human-readable string version of an enum or outputting a value on a per-case basis, can be handled within the enumeration itself.

For example, to create a read-only `numericalLevel` property that returns an integer corresponding to the case, you can create a get method that contains a `switch` statement that switches on the value of `self`. Note that when switching on `self` you don't need to use the member access operator (`.`) at the beginning of the `case` values:

Swift

```swift
var numericalLevel: Int {
    get {
        switch self {
            case Off:
                return 0
            case Min(let level):
                return level
            case Max(let level):
                return level
            case Mid(let minLevel, let maxLevel):
                return (maxLevel - minLevel) / 2
            case Tufnel:
                return 11
        }
    }
}
```

This is very much like defining methods and properties in structures and classes, with one exception: Creating a stored property in an enumeration is not possible.

NESTING TYPES

Much of what has been done to enhance structures and enumerations in Swift has been done in the name of safety and encapsulation. Bringing the functions that act upon structures and enumerations into the types themselves means that the methods and the data they act upon are kept closely tied. Doing this wherever possible makes sense, and Swift gives us yet another opportunity to do so through the availability of nested types.

In Chapter 9, you defined a `VolumeControl` class, which is highly likely to be a consumer of the `VolumeLevel` enumeration.

```Swift
class VolumeControl {
    var volumeLevel: VolumeLevel = VolumeLevel.Off
    //  Remainder of class
}
```

Any other potential "control" classes needing to have an enumeration specific to volume level is unlikely, so nesting the VolumeLevel enumeration inside the VolumeControl class might make sense.

```Swift
class VolumeControl {
    enum VolumeLevel {
        //  Remainder of enumeration
    }

    var volumeLevel: VolumeLevel = VolumeLevel.Off
    //  Remainder of class
}
```

A nested structure or enumeration can still be accessed via their containing type. For example, you could still use VolumeLevel by accessing it this way:

```Swift
var secretVolumeLevel: VolumeControl.VolumeLevel = VolumeControl.VolumeLevel.Off
```

If you want to truly hide your internal implementation, take advantage of Swift's access control and make the nested type private to restrict accessibility to the current file.

WRAPPING UP

The changes made to structures and enumerations in Swift provide many more options to the OS X and iOS developer who cares about the way they craft their code. The ability to add functions to structures and enumerations makes for more readable and logically arranged codebases, and allowing type-safe enumerations that can handle more than just integers makes them easier and safer to use.

In fact, structures have become so much more powerful than strings, and even the native collection types (array and dictionary), have been implemented using them rather than classes. In the next chapter, we will look at memory management in Swift, focusing on the improvements to safety and ease of use it brings over Objective-C.

CHAPTER 11

Memory Management

Perhaps one of the most frustrating aspects of Objective-C in years past was memory management. In the early days, memory management involved manual reference counting—the explicit act of indicating your intention to retain a reference to an object and then release it when you were finished.

Although Apple dabbled with garbage collection in OS X development for a while, reference counting was the only means of memory management for iOS, and it remained popular on OS X. Eventually, automatic reference counting (ARC) was introduced to Objective-C, and although the underlying process was the same, the hard work of deciding when and where to retain and release objects was performed mainly by the compiler rather than the user.

SWIFT MEMORY MANAGEMENT

Thankfully, Swift retains the use of ARC for memory management. In fact, there is some speculation that the introduction of ARC to Objective-C was a happy by-product of its creation for use with Swift. Most of what you know regarding memory management on Swift is the same in Objective-C. The differences involve a refinement of the syntax around closures, and handling of nonoptional values with the unowned reference type, which result in Swift memory management being a little bit safer.

In Objective-C, object references can be one of two types: strong and weak. When you create a strong reference to an object, its *retain* count is increased; the retain count is the total number of strong references for an object. When you create a weak reference (by prefixing a variable declaration with the weak keyword), the retain count is not increased. When you remove a strong reference to an object, its retain count is decreased again. When the retain count becomes zero, it can be deallocated, causing any remaining weak references to the object to be set to `nil`.

Under Swift, the strong reference type (which is still the default) has the same behavior, but an additional measure of complexity is introduced into the mix by optionals. If you were to set up a weak reference to an object using a nonoptional variable type, when the object was deinitialized the weak reference could not be set to `nil`. This means that in Swift you cannot have a weak reference to a nonoptional variable, which can be limiting.

Swift resolves this issue by introducing a new variant on a weak reference: unowned. When you designate a reference as unowned, you are instructing the compiler that you do not want it to be set to `nil` when the object it references has been deinitialized. This means you are able to use nonoptional variables as unowned references.

It also means that you are taking full responsibility for what is done with the variable when the object it references is deinitialized. There is no way to ensure that the object still exists; the reference remains, however, and it can result in a runtime crash if used after the original object is gone.

WHEN TO USE WEAK AND UNOWNED REFERENCES

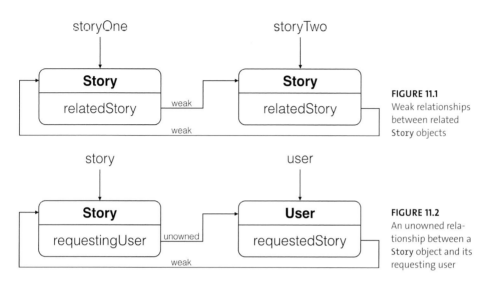

FIGURE 11.1
Weak relationships between related Story objects

FIGURE 11.2
An unowned relationship between a Story object and its requesting user

When you decide to use a weak or an unowned reference, you are making a tradeoff. Using a weak reference means you must use an optional variable, and you need to guard against the variable being `nil` wherever it is used. If you use an unowned reference, you can use a nonoptional variable, yet you take on the extra responsibility of effectively guaranteeing that you will use it wisely, at the risk of a runtime crash.

It is best to use a weak reference to break a potential strong reference cycle whenever that reference does not need to exist for the relationship between two objects to make sense. For example, consider our old friend, the user story. A story could have a `relatedStory` field that links to a second `Story` object; if the second story was also linked to the first, they would cause a strong reference cycle. Since a `relatedStory` is not essential for a user story, these links are best defined as weak references (**Figure 11.1**).

An unowned reference is ideally used when the reference is required for the lifetime of the object. For example, our `Story` object should always have a `requestingUser`—a story cannot exist unless it has been requested by someone. `requestingUser` is defined as an unowned reference, which makes sense because the story can be assumed to have an associated user for its lifetime. On the other hand, a user in the system does not need to have a `requestedStory`, and so this reference should be weak to allow the relationship to be removed at any time (**Figure 11.2**).

> **NOTE:** Remember that these memory management rules are applicable only to reference types. Structures and enumerations are value types and these considerations do not apply to them.

CLOSURES

Both classes and closures are reference types, so when they hold a reference to each other, a strong reference cycle can occur; this can very easily happen if a class defines (and thus holds a reference to) a block, and within the block the code captures a reference to self causing it to be retained. In Objective-C, you often deal with this by creating a weak reference (most often to self) to the object that will be captured by the block. This is a great way to break strong reference cycles but is prone to error; the syntax is nonintuitive, and it is very easy to use a strong reference when the weak reference should have been used instead.

The principle behind avoiding strong reference cycles is similar in Swift, but the syntax differs. Instead of defining a weak reference in the scope that encloses the closure (and being forced to remember to use it), a *capture list* can be defined as part of the closure syntax. The capture list defines any variables that should not be captured as a strong reference. You can continue to refer to the variables by their original name—no more forgetting to type weakSelf!

The syntax for a capture list requires that you supply a variable name, and the type of reference that should be used, within square brackets before the list of parameters in the closure definition:

Swift

```swift
var nonRetainingClosure = {
    [weak self] (name: String) -> (success: Bool) in
    //  Closure body - can reference self with impunity
}
```

The type of reference is required because you can again use weak or unowned reference types as the situation requires, and if you need to include multiple entries in the capture list they should be comma-separated.

WRAPPING UP

Swift takes Objective-C memory management and refines it to make it safer and easier to use. The ability to define capture lists for closures means an end to the ugly pattern of remembering to use `weakSelf`-style variables, while the introduction of the unowned reference type allows the safety of nonoptional variables to be leveraged without strong reference cycles being caused.

In the next chapter, we look at using arrays and dictionaries in detail.

CHAPTER 12

Collections

Contrasting the support for collections between Objective-C and Swift initially seems a little unfair. The collections we know, love, and take for granted in Objective-C (NSArray, NSDictionary, and friends) are actually part of the Foundation framework, which leaves native C arrays as the only direct language-to-language comparison. Given, however, the extent to which the Foundation collections are used in iOS and OS X development, comparing their usage to Swift native collections does make sense.

Swift comes with two native collection types—arrays and dictionaries—and like strings in Swift they can be made immutable by declaring as a constant rather than as a variable. As collections they draw immediate parallels between their Foundation counterparts, though one major Foundation collection without a Swift counterpart is NSSet. Apple might provide a set collection for Swift in the future, but in the meantime, NSSet is never more than an `import Foundation` away.

GENERAL COMPARISONS

A major difference in Swift collections is that they are typed. The methods for inserting and retrieving objects from Foundation collections take the id type, which means that you can insert any type into a collection. This leads to some inconvenience when retrieving objects from the collection; you can either choose to assign directly to the type you *think* the object should be (risking runtime crashes), or you can slip into the common Objective-C pattern of assigning to an id, and then testing for and casting to a specific class type.

Objective-C

```
NSArray *mixedArray = @[@"", @(1)];
id itemOne = mixedArray[0];
if ([itemOne isKindOfClass:NSString]) {
    NSString *itemOneAsString = (NSString *)itemOne;
    // Perform operations on confirmed NSString
}
```

Swift collections are typed by default; if you declare an array as being an array of String objects, the only type you can put into, and thus get out of, that array is a String object. This certainty of what a collection contains means that you don't need extensive guarding when working with the content from a collection, and can only be a good thing.

If you do have a genuine need to work with a mixed type array, other options are still available. If you have a desire to live dangerously and want to create an array containing any type of object, you can use the AnyObject protocol. If you can bear to be a little bit safer, you could instead define your array to take a specific protocol. If you don't care what the actual type is, but know it supports the methods of the protocol, you can handle it a lot more safely. Another alternative is to use generics—both protocols and generics are covered in Chapter 13.

Swift collections can also store "primitive" types directly in an array or dictionary. Foundation collections, however, can store only object types, which means that primitives like integers, floats, or Booleans need to be *boxed* (wrapped in an object type like NSNumber) before they can be inserted into the collection, and *unboxed* when they come out again.

ARRAYS

Arrays are a cornerstone collection type for any programming language. Even little old C had the concept since the beginning. They are a very useful and easy-to-understand concept: a series of *boxes* in memory into which small chunks of data can be placed, replaced, and removed.

Swift arrays are a world apart from C arrays, but are very similar in nature to those provided by Foundation. If anything, given the maturity of Objective-C, Swift's arrays have fewer features, but provide a solid basis for most iOS and OS X development tasks and can be supplemented with NSArray when the need arises.

CREATING ARRAYS

Being native to the Swift standard library, arrays (and dictionaries) have a nice syntax. To declare a new array of a specific type, declare the type inside square brackets. For example to create an array to contain `String` objects, you do this:

```Swift
var stringArray: [String]
```

To initialize an empty array, you do this:

```Swift
stringArray = [String]()
```

Of course, type inference works with array types as well, so you could condense this down to:

```Swift
var inferredStringArray = [String]()
```

Like in Objective-C, you can use a literal syntax to directly populate a new Swift array. To create a new array of `Int` values, you do this:

```Swift
var storyPoints: [Int] = [1, 2, 3, 5, 8]
```

In an attempt to go one better than Objective-C, Swift can also perform type inference from the literal syntax, so this will also work:

```Swift
var inferredStoryPoints = [1, 2, 3, 5, 8]
```

If you want to work with a protocol instead of specific type, you'll need to state the protocol explicitly as a type; Swift is not currently smart enough to infer a common protocol between objects of different types:

```Swift
protocol Estimatable { }
var miscStoryPoints = [Estimatable]()
```

We cover using protocols in further detail in Chapter 13, but this definition allows any type that conforms to the `Estimatable` protocol to be inserted into this array.

READING ARRAY CONTENTS

The easiest way to read a value from an array is to use the familiar square bracket–based literal syntax that was introduced to Objective-C in 2012:

```Swift
let secondItem = storyPoints[1]          // returns 2
```

Just like with `NSArray`, or even with C arrays, bad things can happen if you try to read beyond the end of an array, so be sure you know what size the array is before you start reading at random points. As with `NSArray`, you can call the count property on a Swift array. Keep in mind that arrays are zero-indexed, so you'll need to subtract one from the result to be safe:

```Swift
let arraySize = storyPoints.count        // returns 5
let lastItem = storyPoints[arraySize - 1]  // returns 8
```

Like strings, you can also use the startIndex and endIndex properties if you want to use the advance() function to navigate through an array using indexes, or even use the countElements() function as well.

NOTE: If you want to insert an item at the end of the array, you can use the endIndex property as it is, but if you want to read the last item, you need to advance **backward by one step.**

If you need to get the first or last array elements, you can use the first and last properties, though these return an optional value if the array is empty. If you need to get a slice of some values from the middle of the array, you can take advantage of indexes and range operators:

Swift
```
let firstIndex = advance(storyPoints.startIndex, 1)
let lastIndex = advance(firstIndex, 2)
let subArray = storyPoints[firstIndex...lastIndex]
```

Swift has you covered even if you want a copy of the array in the reverse order:

Swift
```
let backwardsArray = storyPoints.reverse()
```

So far we know how to locate a value in an array based on its index, but what about going the other way around? Sometimes we know, or even just think, an object is in an array, but we don't know its index. Looking at the methods available on the array collection, you would be forgiven for thinking it's just not possible. Thankfully it is possible, but as a global function instead of a method:

Swift
```
let threePointerIndex = find(storyPoints, 3)  // returns 2
```

Unlike NSArray, where if an object can't be found you get the special NSNotFound value, this function returns an optional, which will be nil if the object does not exist in the array, or an Int if it does exist.

MANIPULATING ARRAYS

If you have a mutable array on your hands, you have plenty of facility for adding and removing single or multiple elements at a time. Many of these methods rely on indexes, so make sure you're aware of where you are pointing these operations to avoid runtime crashes.

ADDING OBJECTS
To add a single element to the end of your mutable array—the equivalent of -[NSMutableArray addObject:]—and then call the append method on the array and pass it a new element of the correct type:

Swift
```
storyPoints.append(13)
```

In Objective-C, you can add multiple elements to the end of an array using -[NSMutableArray addObjectsFromArray:]. To achieve the same in Swift, use the extend method with an array of the correct type:

```Swift
let extraPoints = [21, 34]
storyPoints.extend(extraPoints)
```

You can insert elements into an NSMutableArray using -insertObject:atIndex: for a single element, and -insertObjects:atIndexes: for multiple elements. In Swift, inserting a single element uses the insert method:

```Swift
storyPoints.insert(4, atIndex: 3)
```

Unfortunately, when inserting multiple elements, the syntax between Swift and Objective-C differs somewhat. The -insertObjects:atIndexes: takes an array of new objects and an array of indexes that specify where each of the new objects should be inserted. This allows for interweaving the old and new objects where the indexes are not contiguous.

In Swift, you can insert a new sequence of elements only at a single location:

```Swift
let missingPoints = [6, 7]
storyPoints.splice(missingPoints, atIndex: 5)
```

REMOVING OBJECTS

The NSMutableArray type comes with a generous number of ways to remove objects from your array, making Swift seem miserly by comparison. When you want to remove a single object from an array, Swift has you covered. If you know the index, you can extract an object directly:

```Swift
var removedElement = storyPoints.removeAtIndex(3)   // returns 4
```

Unlike its NSMutableArray counterpart, -removeObjectAtIndex:, the removeAtIndex method has the advantage of returning the element that has just been removed. You don't have to use it, but having it available can be handy. The same behavior also applies to Swift's removeLast method, which equates to the -removeLastObject method in NSMutableArray.

```Swift
removedElement = storyPoints.removeLast()          // returns 34
```

An entire group of methods on NSMutableArray have no direct counterparts in the world of Swift—the methods that remove specific objects from an array. For example, the method -removeObject: locates any objects that match (according to an isEqual: comparison) within the array and removes them. The -removeObjectIdenticalTo: method is an alternative that performs the same task but removes only actual instances of the object using a pointer-based match.

To replicate the behavior of -removeObject: in Swift, you can use the find function referenced earlier:

```
if let eightPointerIndex = find(storyPoints, 8) {
    storyPoints.removeAtIndex(eightPointerIndex)
}
```

Note that the find function bases equality on the equals operator (==), so the method -removeObjectIdenticalTo: has no equivalent, which would require an equality based on the identical-to operator (===). Since find cannot narrow its gaze to within a specified range, you cannot directly replicate the methods -removeObject:inRange: or -removeObjectIdenticalTo:inRange:.

To remove multiple objects in one operation, like the -removeObjectsInRange: method on NSMutableArray, you can use the removeRange method in Swift:

```
storyPoints.removeRange(4...5)
```

This method can take only a range, so there is equivalent behavior to that of -removeObjectsAtIndexes: on NSMutableArray.

If you want to use a big-bang approach to object removal, use the removeAll method:

```
storyPoints.removeAll()
```

This method can also be called with a Boolean parameter keepCapacity, which when set to true allows your array to keep the internal capacity it's currently using. If you anticipate reusing the array quite soon at somewhere near its current size, you may want to use true here to improve performance. If you don't need the performance, use false to release the memory instead.

REPLACING OBJECTS

The most direct way to replace an element in an array is to use the subscript assignment operator:

```
storyPoints = [1, 2, 3, 4, 5, 6]
storyPoints[3] = 5
```

You can also use a range operator to replace more than one element. This example replaces the items in the range (4 to 5) with four new elements:

```
storyPoints[4...5] = [8, 9, 10, 11]
```

Note that the number you add does not have to match the number you are replacing. If you want to do a more NSMutableArray-like operation, you can use the replaceRange method:

```
storyPoints.replaceRange(5...7, with:[13, 21])
```

SORTING

Objective-C gives you numerous methods to sort arrays, and your preferred means of doing so may actually be a clue to how long you've been working with the language. As it has evolved, new array-sorting methods have been introduced, and they range from passing a pointer to a sort function, to passing a collection of sort descriptors, to supplying a comparator block. If you're a fan of anything but the last method, you may be disappointed with Swift.

Swift does retain Objective-C's method of differentiating between sorting an array in-place (using the sort method), and producing a sorted copy from an array that is left untouched (using the sorted method). Of course, if your array is a constant, it can offer only the sorted method.

Both methods use the same general syntax to perform their actions: The method is passed a function or closure that takes two parameters and returns a Boolean. A return value of true indicates that the first parameter should appear before the second parameter in the sorted output, false indicates that the second parameter should appear before the first.

```swift
func descendingSort(first: Int, second: Int) -> Bool {
    return first > second
}
storyPoints.sort(descendingSort)
```
Swift

Because the method takes a closure as a parameter, you can take advantage of trailing closure syntax and shorthand parameter names to condense sort operations:

```swift
let ascendingPoints = storyPoints.sorted { $0 < $1 }
```
Swift

DICTIONARIES

In the world of C, arrays were deemed all that was necessary for collections. Just remember the index of every element, and the entire collection was at your disposal. But as data become more structured, voluminous, and complex, the concept of dictionaries (or hash maps) would obviously become more important. The Swift standard library naturally should include a dictionary collection as part of the bare minimum functionality for the language.

When defined as a constant, the Swift dictionary is equivalent to NSDictionary in Foundation, and when created as a variable it takes on the role of NSMutableDictionary (though for the sake of brevity we'll just refer to both as NSDictionary from here on).

CREATING DICTIONARIES

To create and initialize a dictionary in one fell swoop, specify the key and value types inside square brackets (like an overstuffed array syntax) separated by a colon:

```swift
var translationDictionary = [String: String]()
```
Swift

The first of the two types is the key type, and the second is the value type. Here you're using a String as both key and value types, but they don't have to be the same. You can populate a dictionary using literal syntax, which differs slightly from Objective-C syntax in that it uses square brackets instead of curly brackets:

Swift

```
translationDictionary = [
    "favorite": "favourite",
    "color": "colour",
    "initializer": "initialiser",
    "parentheses": "round brackets",
    "pound sign": "hash",
    "behavior": "behaviour"
]
```

As with arrays, you can use type inference when creating a dictionary using literal syntax.

READING FROM DICTIONARIES

You can obtain a single value from a dictionary using the subscript operator along with a key:

Swift

```
var realWord = translationDictionary["color"] //  returns optional containing
→ "colour"
```

Unlike an array, fetching a value from a dictionary returns an optional value (in this case String?). Due to the arbitrary nature of keys, it's much more likely that a lookup will result in the dictionary having no entry for a supplied key. This is very similar to the behavior of the subscript operator, valueForKey:, and objectForKey: with NSDictionary.

As with NSDictionary, the ordering of items within a Swift dictionary is seemingly random, so while you can iterate over dictionary items in a number of ways, doing so doesn't always make sense. If you do need to iterate through a dictionary, accessing both the keys and values, Objective-C requires the following pattern:

Objective-C

```
for (NSString *key in translationDictionary) {
    NSString *value = translationDictionary[key];
    NSLog(@"%@: %@", key, value);
}
```

Swift on the other hand can iterate over a dictionary and return a tuple like this:

Swift

```
for (key, value) in translationDictionary {
    println("\(key): \(value)")
}
```

If you want a list of just the keys or the values, you can use read-only properties on the dictionary type just like allKeys or allValues on NSDictionary, though these are different in that they are not returned as plain arrays. They can be iterated and accessed using the subscript operator but must use an index value obtained from the dictionary itself.

This is similar to accessing a character within a string. You can obtain an index relating to the start or end of the dictionary using the startIndex and endIndex properties. You can also get the index that corresponds to a key (although it will return an optional that needs to be unwrapped if it is not nil):

```
var keyIndex = translationDictionary.indexForKey("pound sign")
if let validKeyIndex = keyIndex {
    realWord = translationDictionary.values[validKeyIndex]   // returns "hash"
}
```
Swift

MANIPULATING DICTIONARIES

As long as you have a variable reference to a dictionary, you can make changes to its contents.

ADDING AND REPLACING OBJECTS

Adding and/or replacing items in a dictionary is as straightforward as using the subscript assignment operator. If an object corresponding to the supplied key already exists in the dictionary, it will be replaced; if the key doesn't already exist, it will be added instead:

```
translationDictionary.count                             // returns 6
translationDictionary["Apple has"] = "Apple have"
translationDictionary.count                             // returns 7
translationDictionary["pound sign"] = "octothorpe"
translationDictionary.count                             // returns 7
```
Swift

If you need to know whether an insertion succeeded without wanting to check the before and after count values, use the dictionary method updateValue(value:forKey:). It returns an optional containing the replaced value, or nil if no value already existed for the key:

```
let oldWord = translationDictionary.updateValue("coloUr", forKey: "color")
→ // returns "colour"
```
Swift

REMOVING OBJECTS

To remove a single key and its associated value from a dictionary, use:

```
let removedWord = translationDictionary.removeValueForKey("Apple has")
```
Swift

Like updating a value for a key, this method returns an optional value containing the removed item if the key exists, and nil if the key doesn't exist. If you have an index instead of a key, you can use it instead:

```
let index = translationDictionary.startIndex
translationDictionary.removeAtIndex(index)
```
Swift

Be careful doing this—making sure the index is valid is up to you. If the index goes out of range, a runtime crash will occur. This method also doesn't give back the value removed, so it is easily the least useful option.

When you want to clear out your dictionary completely (for example, if you're finished converting a UK author's text to US English), you can do so with removeAll. As with arrays, removeAll can take a Boolean parameter that allows you to keep or remove the current capacity of the dictionary.

```
translationDictionary.removeAll()
```

MUTABILITY

Taking time to consider matters of mutability is worthwhile when discussing the Swift collection types because they differ slightly from those in Objective-C.

In Objective-C, we consider an array to be mutable if it is declared as an NSMutableArray and immutable if it is an NSArray. It's right there in the name, and so when you pass a mutable array into a method in Objective-C, you can expect to be able to add elements to it. Consider the following method:

```
- (void)mutatingTheArray:(NSMutableArray *)theArray {
    [theArray addObject:@"Another Object"];
}
```

When this method is called, the mutable array is updated even in the calling code. Consider the same method in Swift however:

```
var mutableArray = [1, 2, 3, 4]
func mutatingTheArray(theArray: [Int]) {
    theArray.append(5)
}
```

Unfortunately, this produces the error shown in **Figure 12.1**.

You may remember from the function parameter discussion in Chapter 6 that passed parameters are constants by default, so you cannot modify this parameter without declaring it as a variable.

Yet another difference between Objective-C and Swift raises its head at this point. In Objective-C, arrays and dictionaries are implemented as class object types; in Swift they are implemented as structure object types. In Chapter 10, we learned that structures were copied when they were assigned or passed into functions; when you pass mutableArray into the function, what you actually get access to in the function is a copy of mutableArray. You can make as many changes as you like, but the changes will be discarded when the function completes and the passed parameter goes out of scope.

```
161   var mutableArray = [1, 2, 3, 4]
162   func mutatingTheArray(theArray: [Int]) {
 63       theArray.append(5)
164   }                      ❶ Immutable value of type '[Int]' only has mutating members named 'append'
```

FIGURE 12.1 Unsuccessfully trying to mutate an array

The best way to modify an array or dictionary is to pass it to a function, make changes to the copy, return the copy, and assign it back to the original collection:

```swift
func mutatingTheArray(var theArray: [Int]) -> [Int] {
    theArray.append(5)
    return theArray
}


mutableArray = mutatingTheArray(mutableArray)
```

Swift

WRAPPING UP

Compared to the Foundation collection classes, the Swift native collections may seem to be lacking in both range and functionality. Foundation does have many more collection types, and the NSArray and NSDictionary classes have a larger choice of methods. However, Swift brings something new to the table in the form of strongly typed collections that work directly with all the native Swift types, making them safer and more convenient. Swift collections also provide a solid foundation for much more to come.

In the next chapter we look at protocols and extensions, the Swift equivalent of Objective-C's categories. We also look at generics, a natural progression from both protocols and categories/extensions that has never been available to iOS and OS X developers before.

CHAPTER 13

Protocols, Extensions, and Generics

Protocols should be a familiar sight to any Objective-C developer. They are used throughout the Apple frameworks to define behaviors (in the form of properties and methods) that classes should conform to. Although extensions may sound new, they already exist in Objective-C as categories and can be used to provide extra functionality to existing classes. Swift protocols and extensions differ from their Objective-C counterparts in that they can be used with structures and enumerations as well as classes.

Generics are a completely new technology introduced by Swift. Their purpose is to allow a function or a type to be created in such a way that the type it acts upon does not need to be specified at compile time. This makes the function or type usable with a wider range of types, and thus generic in nature. Arrays and dictionaries in Swift rely upon generics to be strongly typed; without generics the Swift developers would have to create a variant of the array and dictionary type to handle every possible type combination, as well as predict every type you will ever create.

PROTOCOLS

Protocols behave in much the same way in Swift as they do in Objective-C, with the major differences lying in the syntax for creating and conforming to them. Swift protocols can be used with classes, structures, and even enumerations.

CREATING

The Objective-C syntax for defining a protocol is similar to that for defining interface and implementation blocks. The protocol name is on a line following the @protocol keyword, and the definition is concluded with the @end keyword:

Objective-C

```
@protocol Estimatable
//  Method or property declarations
@end
```

Defining a protocol in Swift is very similar to object type definition where the protocol keyword is followed by the name and a pair of curly braces delimiting the protocol block: protocol Estimatable { ... }.

Protocols can inherit from one or more other protocols, allowing the combination of their requirements into a single protocol:

Swift

```
protocol Predictable: Estimatable, Guessable { ... }
```

Restricting a protocol to be adopted by only class types is possible by using the keyword class as though inheriting from another protocol:

Swift

```
protocol ClassyProtocol: class { ... }
```

METHODS

Including a method in a protocol is the same as defining a method in any of the object types but without the need to include the body or the curly braces:

Swift

```
protocol Estimatable {
    func produceValidEstimate(guess: Int) -> Int
    func decreaseEstimate()
}
```

If the method causes member data to be modified in any way, the method must be marked with the mutating keyword. Although class types do not need the mutating keyword, it should be included if the protocol (**Figure 13.1**) is to be adopted by a structure or enumeration.

```
13   protocol Estimatable {
14       func decreaseEstimate()
15   }
16
❶17   struct StoryPoint: Estimatable {
18       var estimate: Int = 0        ❶ Type 'StoryPoint' does not conform to protocol 'Estimatable'
19       mutating func decreaseEstimate() {
20           if estimate > 0 { estimate-- }
21       }
22   }
```

FIGURE 13.1 A structure cannot conform to a protocol when the mutating keyword has not been included.

Although you can define default values for function parameters in Swift, you can't specify a default value in a protocol definition. Make sure your parameter names (internal and external) are correct; they must match exactly between protocol and implementation.

To create a type method (an Objective-C class method) as part of a protocol, use the keyword class. When implementing the type method in a structure or enumeration, you must redefine the method with the keyword static.

PROPERTIES

Defining a property in a protocol is similar to defining a property for object types, but doing so requires that you specify if it should just have a getter method, or should also have a setter method:

```
protocol Estimatable {
    var maximumValue: Int { get }
    var estimate: Int { get set }
}
```

If the protocol specifies get set, your implementing type must provide the same property with both getter and setter methods; a variable stored property or a computed property with a getter and a setter would satisfy this requirement.

However, if the protocol specifies get, your implementing type must provide the same property with a getter method *at a minimum*; a constant stored property, a variable stored property, a computed property with just a getter, or a computed property with a getter and a setter would all satisfy this requirement.

> **NOTE:** Properties must always be declared as var in the protocol, even if you do not intend to use them as a variable in the conforming type. When you implement a protocol, you are free to redefine the property as a constant if you wish.

Unlike in Objective-C, you can create type properties in a Swift protocol by prefixing the property definition with the keyword class. As with type methods, when implementing the protocol for a structure or enumeration, you must redefine a type property with the static keyword.

OPTIONAL METHODS AND PROPERTIES

Just like Objective-C, Swift has support for defining both methods and properties as optional requirements for a protocol. In both cases the protocol definition needs to be preceded by the keyword optional—unlike Objective-C where a single @optional statement indicates that each method or property definition that follows is optional.

Unfortunately, optional methods and properties can be used only if your protocol is annotated with the @objc attribute. Using this attribute restricts your implementing type to only classes (as though you specified the class keyword while defining your protocol). For more information on the @objc attribute, see Chapter 15.

CONFORMING TO PROTOCOLS

To conform to a protocol with an object type, the protocol must be listed in the same way that you would implement inheritance for a class type:

Swift

```swift
struct StoryPoint: Estimatable {
    var maximumValue: Int {
        return 5
    }
    var estimate: Int = 0
    func produceValidEstimate(guess: Int) -> Int {
        return estimate
    }
    mutating func decreaseEstimate() {
        if estimate > 0 { estimate-- }
    }
}
```

NOTE: Unlike in Objective-C, non-conformance to a protocol is actually a compiler error in Swift.

An object type can conform to multiple protocols by stating the protocol types separated by commas. Classes that inherit from a base class must specify the base class before any protocols it intends to conform to.

Objective-C indicates that a variable or method parameter should conform to a protocol by stating a type (often id) followed by the protocol within angle brackets: id<Estimatable> estimatableItem. In Swift, a protocol is considered to be a type without an actual implementation, so declaring it as a type without angle brackets is sufficient: var estimatableItem: Estimatable.

The exception to this is when a constant or variable should conform to multiple protocols—known as *protocol composition*. To achieve this, use the keyword protocol followed by the protocol names separated by commas, within angle brackets:

```
var estimatableGuessableItem: protocol<Estimatable, Guessable>
```

Unfortunately, if you are working with classes and need to take inheritance into account (like using UIViewController<UITableViewDataSource> in Objective-C), you may be disappointed because this kind of construct is not available.

To determine if an object type conforms to a protocol, you can use Swift's *type operators* (although only if your protocol is marked with the @objc attribute). The is operator substitutes for the isKindOfClass: and conformsToProtocol: reflection methods defined in the NSObject protocol. If you are satisfied that an object conforms to a protocol, you can use the as operator to downcast an object to a protocol, or you can use as? to optionally downcast.

Similarly, you can test for optional conformance to a protocol by treating an optional method or parameter like an optional value; this allows for handling using optional chaining or optional binding.

EXTENSIONS

In Objective-C, classes can have their functionality increased by creating a *category* on them. The class could rely on this functionality being available anywhere the category was imported, making it a useful way to add convenience methods to existing types, even those that belonged to third-party developers. This is a useful alternative to using inheritance to add functionality to a class.

Swift retains the capabilities of categories under the new name of *extensions*, and extends their functionality to structures and enumerations as well. An extension can be used to introduce new instance and type methods, add new computed properties (both instance and type), and store type properties.

To create an extension for an existing type, use the keyword extension followed by the type name and a block enclosed in curly braces that contains the properties and methods to be added by the extension:

```
extension StoryPoint {
    mutating func managerOverride() {
        decreaseEstimate()
    }
}
```

> **NOTE:** Unlike Objective-C categories, extensions do not get named, so documenting their purpose through comments in your code is helpful.

Extensions can also be added within the same source file as the object type it extends. You can take advantage of this to use extensions to split up your type into logical blocks. It's even possible to apply access control to an extension; you can use this to create "blocks" of private methods and properties without having to individually declare them as private.

An extension can also add protocol conformance to an existing type by stating the protocol name and implementing the required methods as part of the extension body: extension StoryPoint: Guessable { ... }. Because you can extend any object type, including framework-supplied types, you can use this technique to make any other type conform to your protocols.

GENERICS

Swift's introduction of generics to OS X and iOS development was somewhat divisive. Generics are a powerful feature of any language, and it's fair to say that many developers have both benefitted and been burned by that power. Generics give you the ability to create functions and types that can be used with a variety of other object types. This makes creating reusable code easier, but it can also make for code that is harder to debug.

GENERIC FUNCTIONS

To define a generic function, add a *type parameter* inside angle brackets to the end of the function name but before the opening parenthesis. A type parameter is a placeholder parameter you will use in your function definition and body to represent any type passed to the function. It is often represented by the letter T but feel free to make it more descriptive. You can use multiple type parameters by separating them with commas.

The following example creates a function named arrayicize that takes a single parameter and returns it within a typed array. The passed parameter is of type T, and it returns an array of type T. The function body creates the array with a type of T, adds the passed parameter, and returns it:

Swift

```swift
func arrayicize<T>(type: T) -> [T] {
    var arrayOfType: [T] = [type]
    return arrayOfType
}
arrayicize(1)        // returns [ 1 ]
arrayicize("One")    // returns [ "One" ]
```

GENERIC TYPES

Generic types are often used to provide custom collection types to a language; Swift arrays and dictionaries are themselves implemented as structures with the aid of generics. To create a generic type, simply state the object type as normal, but add one or more type parameters within angle brackets at the end of the type name, and before listing any types to inherit or protocols to conform to.

In the following code example, you create a generic type for estimating point values based on user stories (a means of describing product functionality in an agile software development workflow). The type parameter T can represent any point type (or any type really) and store them as an array ([T]()). The estimator can be populated with story points using the addPoint() method, which receives the generic type T. Once populated, you can supply a user story for the estimator to evaluate (estimateFromUserStory()), and then return a story point value. If the estimator is not populated, the method returns an optional T?.

Swift

```Swift
class PointEstimator <T> {
    private var points = [T]()
    func addPoint(point: T) { points.append(point) }
    func estimateFromUserStory(story: String) -> T? {
        let i = arc4random_uniform(UInt32(points.count))
        return points[Int(i)]
    }
}
```

Instantiating a generic type is similar to the normal instantiation process, but the internal type (or types) should be specified in angle brackets after the generic type name. Don't worry, it sounds more complex than it looks:

Swift

```Swift
var estimator = PointEstimator<StoryPoint>()
estimator.addPoint(StoryPoint(estimate: 0))
estimator.addPoint(StoryPoint(estimate: 1))
estimator.addPoint(StoryPoint(estimate: 2))
estimator.addPoint(StoryPoint(estimate: 3))
estimator.estimateFromUserStory("User story")   //  returns random value!
```

While the estimator example is living proof that engineers create estimates at random, it suffers a flaw in that it allows any type to be handled. You want your code to be generic, but sometimes not too generic; you could create an estimator that takes UIView objects, but would that really make sense?

Fortunately, generics support the concept of type constraints. These allow specification of a type parameter but at the same time narrowing down the range of types that can qualify for use. To do this, place a colon after the type parameter, and specify one or more protocols as the type constraints:

```
class StoryPointEstimator <T: Estimatable> { ... }
```

If you use multiple protocols as a type constraint, only types that conform to *all the protocols* will be accepted as a valid type parameter.

WRAPPING UP

Swift provides more functionality than we've ever had before for customizing types in iOS and OS X development. Protocols are more powerful than ever; extensions have extended the capabilities of classes, structures, and enumerations alike; and generics provide us with new ways to build our own generic types—an essential feature in any modern, type-safe language.

In the next chapter we'll look at some other new features of Swift that have no equivalents in Objective-C, and also some features of Objective-C that unfortunately have been left behind in the transition to Swift.

CHAPTER 14

There Isn't a Word for That

Try as Apple might, Swift was never going to be a complete feature-for-feature replacement for Objective-C in its first few releases. Conversely, Swift could never be seen as a truly modern language if it simply imitated the Objective-C feature set with only a new syntax. As a result, this chapter takes a look at some of the features left behind in the transition from Swift to Objective-C, as well as some of the new features in Swift we haven't had a chance to delve into yet.

ONLY IN OBJECTIVE-C

The transition to any new programming language will always have an inevitable backlash regarding functionality perceived to be missing. The migration from Objective-C to Swift is no exception. The Swift developers have not indicated if these omissions were made simply because of time constraints, or if they were instead conscious decisions to move away from features they considered no longer essential. In some cases, you'll need to fall back to Objective-C classes for the missing functionality; in others you'll need to find alternative ways to achieve the same results.

EXCEPTION HANDLING

Many developers consider exceptions and exception handling to be an essential part of any modern programming language, yet they are conspicuously absent in Swift. How strongly a developer feels about the lack of exception handling will vary with their programming philosophy and history. Some developers favor using exceptions only in the most *exceptional* circumstances, while others prefer using exceptions as an alternative form of flow control.

The best advice is to move away from throwing exceptions in any Objective-C code that could potentially be used in a project with Swift code. Where you currently use exceptions for flow control, try migrating toward an NSError-style approach, where you pass back an error object rather than throwing an exception. You can of course use NSError itself or create your own equivalent; or you can choose whether to use inout parameters or to return errors from functions as part of a tuple.

Where you use exceptions in truly exceptional circumstances, you could instead use an *assertion*, a means to terminate your application. Swift provides two ways to include an assertion in your application:

- The assert() function takes a conditional statement and an optional message. If the condition evaluates to false, the assertion stops the application and logs the message.
- The assertFailure() function takes an optional message and when reached stops the application.

Assertions are not executed in optimized builds and are not intended for shipping in a production build of your app. Ideally, all circumstances that would cause an assertion to be executed will have been identified in prerelease testing.

KVO

Key-value observing (KVO) is a heavily used Objective-C feature that allows one object to observe changes in the state of another object and react to those changes. This feature is immensely useful, and its omission from Swift is a blow for those who heavily use it.

If your observation needs are not extensive and are known in advance, property observers are an alternative. This basic form of observation is built right into the Swift object type syntax to allow your code to react to changes in its own properties. For more information, see the "Property Observers" section in Chapter 9.

KVO is not completely gone; if your Swift class inherits from NSObject, you can still take advantage of it. In a class you want to observe, mark any properties you want to observe with the dynamic keyword. Unlike in pure Objective-C, where any property can be observed, the dynamic keyword is essential when performing KVO from Swift.

You'll also need to create a *global context variable*; the type is unimportant, it just needs to be visible from the code that sets up the observer, and from the code that is doing the observing. In your observer class, use addObserver(forKeyPath:options:context:) to set up the observer, and override the observeValueForKeyPath(ofObject:change:context:) method as you normally would in Objective-C, making sure to use the global context variable for the context parameter.

REFLECTION

Reflection is the ability of a piece of code to "inspect" aspects of itself. Objective-C provides reflection through methods provided by NSObject (for example, -respondsToSelector:) or from the underlying runtime (for example, requesting the names of ivars, or selectors available in a class).

As you might expect, some degree of reflection is available if your classes inherit from NSObject. Otherwise you are limited to some undocumented functions that seem to be provided mainly for the purposes of Xcode support. Reflection support will likely improve in Swift but may not be up to par with Objective-C for some time.

> **TIP:** To see the current state of reflection support, enter MirrorType into a playground, and Command-click it to see what methods it provides.

DYNAMIC DISPATCH

Dynamic dispatch is the name given to the mechanism by which Objective-C methods are called. At runtime the selector of the method is looked up from a list to determine where to find the code that should be run. Objective-C developers have taken advantage of numerous dynamic dispatch shenanigans over the years, such as intercepting method invocation to handle unimplemented selectors or swapping out method implementations at runtime (a process known as *swizzling*).

Pure Swift code uses different mechanisms—known as *static* or *vtable dispatch*—for determining the code to run when a method is called. This mechanism is much faster than dynamic dispatch, but precludes the ability to intercept a method invocation at runtime, or changing entries in the dispatch table to perform swizzling. If this behavior is important to you, methods marked with the dynamic keyword will be forced into using dynamic dispatch at runtime at a potential performance cost. Be aware that marking a method with the @objc attribute provides only a hint to the compiler that dynamic dispatch should be used; the dynamic keyword mandates it.

NEW TO SWIFT

We've already covered a number of new Swift features during the course of this book (such as tuples, generics, access controls, and the enhanced capabilities of structures and enumerations), but we simply haven't gotten around to some of them yet.

NAMESPACES

Most Objective-C developers are familiar with class prefixing: that ancient art of carefully choosing a three-letter (or two if you were naughty) combination that represented yourself or your company so that your class names didn't clash with those created by Apple or other developers.

Swift introduces the concept of namespaces to reduce the chances of conflict between your type names and those from other developers. Even better, you don't need to do much to take advantage of this feature because all code is namespaced on a per-module basis, and modules are defined based on their Xcode targets.

To use code from another module/namespace, you need to `import` only the module name; Foundation, AppKit, and UIKit are all imported in this way. Once imported, the types in a module can be accessed directly using just their type names.

In the event that a conflict occurs between a type in your module and another framework, you can use the fully qualified name to access the type from the framework (for example, `UIKit.UIView`), and the type name on its own will access the type within your module. If you encounter a conflict between two external frameworks, use the fully qualified names to distinguish between them.

CUSTOM OPERATORS

As developers, we all enjoy the freedoms that come with naming our functions and types however we like, but for the operators we use in interacting with our types we have long been confined to those prescribed by Objective-C.

Some projects—particularly in the realms of math, science, engineering, or finance— may benefit from being able to create their own operators to represent common operations specific to the project domain.

For example, consider a writer who needs to know how many pages a certain word count equates to. The simplest calculation is to divide the word count by an average number of words per page. Given that books contain whole numbers of pages, the result should be rounded up. You could do this the long way using the `ceil()` standard library function. Instead, you'll define a new operator that represents "divide and round up":

Swift

```
infix operator /^ { associativity left precedence 100 }
func /^ (left: Double, right: Double) -> Int {
    return Int(ceil(left / right))
}
```

The first line defines the operator type (we have used `infix`, but it can also be `prefix` or `postfix`), the operator itself, and a set of curly braces defining any parameters required for the operator. In the case of `infix` operators, you define the `associativity` and `precedence` values required for interacting with other operators. You can use the operator like this:

```
let pageCount = 3100 /^ 250      //  returns 13
```

> **TIP:** An extensive collection of mathematical operators has already been created by Mattt Thompson. The Euler project on GitHub (https://github.com/mattt/Euler) is a great way to learn about custom operators.

In the never-ending quest to make code unmaintainable, few tools are as useful in your armory as operator overloading. Swift not only allows you to define your own custom operators, but you can also take the system-supplied operators and redefine them for your own nefarious purposes.

Operator overloading can be very effective when used in moderation (for example, adding an operator to combine your own custom types), but it should be carried out with caution. Redefining an existing operator with subtly different behavior can lead to confusion for other developers and create hard-to-track-down bugs.

Consider the `StoryPoint` structure from Chapter 13. If you wanted to combine two story point estimates, you would have to extract the estimate values, add them, and create a new story point object with the estimate total. You could encapsulate this with an overloaded + operator like this:

```
func + (left: StoryPoint, right: StoryPoint) -> StoryPoint {
    return StoryPoint(estimate: (left.estimate + right.estimate))
}
let onePointer = StoryPoint(estimate: 1)
let twoPointer = StoryPoint(estimate: 2)
let threePointer = onePointer + twoPointer
```

Swift

FILTER, MAP, AND REDUCE

If you've spent any time with developers from outside the world of Objective-C and Cocoa, you're bound to have heard them discuss strange and exotic topics like functional programming, higher-order functions, and map reducing.

When Swift was announced, Apple emphasized that it would be more favorable toward the concepts of functional programming, especially because using functions as parameters was now possible. A full discussion of functional programming in Swift is the subject for another book, but three Swift functions that have been directly inspired by first-class functions in other programming languages are worth discussing: `filter`, `map`, and `reduce`.

These functions share a common pattern in that they take (or can be called upon) a set of data and a function that should be used to act on that data, producing a modified set of data that is returned.

To provide a usable (if trivial) example, you will continue to use the concept of user stories and their points values. Here you define a class named Story that holds a name and a point value, and define an array named currentStories to hold some data for later processing.

Swift

```swift
class Story {
    let name: String
    var point: StoryPoint
    init(_ name: String, _ point: StoryPoint) {
        self.name = name
        self.point = point
    }
}
let currentStories = [
    Story("Story 1", StoryPoint(estimate: 3)),
    Story("Story 2", StoryPoint(estimate: 1)),
    Story("Story 3", StoryPoint(estimate: 4)),
    Story("Story 4", StoryPoint(estimate: 1)),
    Story("Story 5", StoryPoint(estimate: 3)),
    Story("Story 6", StoryPoint(estimate: 2)),
    Story("Story 7", StoryPoint(estimate: 0)),
    Story("Story 8", StoryPoint(estimate: 1))
]
```

What you want from this data is an accumulated total of the stories that have point values between 1 and 3. You don't care about stories with 0 or 4 points, and you don't care about the story names. The logical first step is to discard the unnecessary stories (those with 0 or 4 points), so you need a way to filter these out.

FILTER

A filtering operation can be carried out in Swift by calling the global filter function. This function is passed a collection to be filtered and a filtering function, which can be defined as a function or a closure. To process the data set, you will apply a filter that removes stories with point values less than 1 and point values greater than 3. To do this, you pass currentStories to the filter function, and follow it with a filtering operation using trailing closure syntax.

Swift

```swift
let filteredStories = filter(currentStories) { (story: Story) -> Bool in
    return story.point.estimate > 0 && story.point.estimate < 4
}
filteredStories.count          //  returns 6
```

This will filter out two of the array elements, leaving six remaining. From this reduced data set, you want to transform the Story objects into a set of corresponding integers that can be summed at a later stage.

MAP

The map function can be used to perform a transform operation; an input collection is passed through a supplied mapping function to produce an output collection. The mapping function you are going to supply in the following code takes a Story as an input and extracts the estimate value from its point object. The integer is then returned from the closure, for the map function to place it into the output collection.

Swift

```swift
let pointsOnly = map(filteredStories) { (story: Story) -> Int in
    let point = story.point
    return point.estimate
}
```

This leaves you with an array of integer values (pointsOnly) ready to be summed to produce the total amount of story points.

REDUCE

A reducing function is intended to take a collection of data and reduce it down to a single value. The Swift reduce function takes an input collection, a starting value, and a closure that is used to perform the reduction. The closure itself takes two parameters: The first is a running total, and the second is the next value from the input collection. The closure returns a new integer value, which is then fed back into the next iteration. When the reduce function runs out of data to reduce, it returns the total back to be assigned to totalPoints.

Swift

```swift
let totalPoints = reduce(pointsOnly, 0) { (subtotal: Int, nextValue: Int) ->
→ Int in
        return subtotal + nextValue
}
totalPoints        //  returns 11
```

This has been a simple example, but hopefully one that illustrates the potential that filter, map, and reduce could have for your code.

WRAPPING UP

Swift is a quickly evolving new language. It clearly will be the future of OS X and iOS development, and the best way to shape that future is to get involved in the process. During its beta phase, numerous improvements were added and fixes made as a direct result of user feedback. If you are a registered developer, you can log in to the Bug Reporter tool (http://bugreport.apple.com) and raise a problem request to report an issue or suggest a potential improvement.

In the next chapter we look further at how to interact between the two languages, allowing you to leverage your existing Objective-C codebase with new code you write in Swift.

CHAPTER 15

Interacting with Objective-C

The future for OS X and iOS development very clearly lies in Swift. Given that it's a completely new language, and Cocoa development is so closely tied to Objective-C, convincing developers to move across completely without ensuring some level of interoperability would never have been an easy task.

Fortunately, the level of integration between the two languages can be adjusted to suit the individual developer or organization. You can selectively introduce Swift classes to an existing Objective-C project, or include entire Swift-based frameworks, allowing you to start small and introduce greater amounts of Swift code as time goes on.

Conversely, if you want to start new projects in Swift, yet still leverage your existing Objective-C code in the form of individual classes or frameworks (third party or your own), plenty of options are available.

INTRODUCING SWIFT TO OBJECTIVE-C

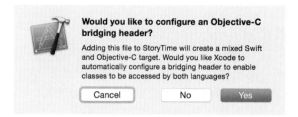

Many developers will have no option but to introduce Swift to their existing Objective-C code; the time or financial budget may not be available to switch everything to another language in one fell swoop. Apple's "mix and match" approach to using Swift is ideal here; you can selectively introduce Swift code on a file-by-file basis or as a complete framework.

ADDING SWIFT FILES

When working with an existing Objective-C project, adding Swift code is a simple process. Choose File > New > File. In the template dialog, select the Swift File template, and give your new file a name and location. With this action, you'll be creating a "mixed target" consisting of both Objective-C and Swift code, so Xcode will display a new dialog asking if you want to create a *bridging header* (**Figure 15.1**).

Clicking Yes will cause Xcode to create the bridging header. Any Objective-C classes in the current target you would like to be able to access from your Swift code should be "imported" into this file. If you intend your code to "flow" only one way—using Swift in Objective-C but not the other way around—you don't need a bridging header and can click No. That said, little is lost by creating one now—the choice is completely yours.

NOTE: The process is the same whether you create the Swift files from a template, or drag and drop existing files into your project. Xcode will detect that you are adding Swift code and display the same prompt.

Swift doesn't have header files, so Xcode doesn't need to create a visible bridging header equivalent for the reverse operation. However, some means to expose Swift types to Objective-C is still needed.

FIGURE 15.2 Locating the Swift header for Objective-C using Open Quickly

USING SWIFT CODE IN OBJECTIVE-C

Objective-C does not understand Swift code without a little bit of your help. When you compile Swift source files in a mixed language target, the compiler will output a header file containing Objective-C representations of any Swift classes you wish to use from your Objective-C code.

If you want a Swift class to be recognized by Objective-C, it needs to be marked with the @objc attribute. This attribute causes a Swift class and its public and internal methods and properties to be included in the Swift header. The header can then be imported by your Objective-C code, and Swift objects can then be used as though they were written in Objective-C all along. You must use the syntax #import "*ModuleName*-Swift.h" when trying to perform an import.

> **NOTE:** The Swift header does not exist within your project source code, but you can still view it by using the Open Quickly feature (Command-Shift-O) and typing the name of your module (Figure 15.2).

The @objc attribute can also be added to protocols, extensions, methods, and properties, but it cannot be added to structures or enumerations (the second-class citizens of the Objective-C world). If you include one of these types as a property, a parameter, or a return value, it will not be included in the Swift header.

You can implicitly apply the @objc attribute in a number of ways. Extending a class from NSObject, or a class that indirectly inherits from NSObject, will have the same effect as @objc. Marking a method or property with the keyword dynamic, or with the attributes @IBOutlet or @IBAction, or with the @NSManaged attribute (indicating a Core Data managed object) will do the same.

When you make a change to your Swift code, be sure to perform an Xcode build action. The Swift header file is not automatically generated; it requires a build to be performed for any changes to be made available to the Objective-C code.

Instantiating a Swift class is done in the same way as a regular Objective-C class but with a small caveat: If you have just added @objc to your class, you won't be able to take advantage of the alloc class method. The two ways around this limitation are to either inherit from NSObject or define a convenience method for creating an object:

Swift

```
@objc class StoryPoint {
    class func createStoryPoint() -> StoryPoint {
        return StoryPoint()
    }
}
```

Then in your Objective-C code, you can create the object like this:

```
StoryPoint *storyPoint = [StoryPoint createStoryPoint];
```

When generating the Swift header, Xcode will do its best to make your Swift initializers as much like Objective-C as possible. For example, with the initializer `init(estimate:Int)`, the generated Objective-C initializer becomes `-initWithEstimate:(NSInteger)estimate`.

Xcode does not make your regular Swift methods Objective-C-like, but if you wish to customize a method name, the `@objc` attribute can be supplied with a parameter to override the default method name created by Xcode. If you wanted to supply an initial value to `createStoryPoint()`, you could do the following:

```
@objc(createStoryPointWithEstimate:)
class func createStoryPoint(estimate:Int) -> StoryPoint {
    return StoryPoint(estimate: estimate)
}
```

If for some reason the generated initializers don't suit your taste, this technique can also be used to customize the initializer names as well.

USING OBJECTIVE-C WITH SWIFT

Even if you do have the freedom to immediately switch to using Swift full time, you'll probably need to reuse some Objective-C code somewhere in your projects. Of course, both AppKit and UIKit are still firmly based on Objective-C, and if you use third-party code you have less say in when it migrates to Swift.

ADDING OBJECTIVE-C FILES

The process for adding Objective-C files to a Swift project is much the same as that for the reverse procedure discussed in the previous section. When creating, or importing, an Objective-C class, Xcode will display the same prompt to create a bridging header (Figure 15.1).

The bridging header filename takes the format *ModuleName*-Bridging-Header.h, and unlike its Swift counterpart, it appears as a file in the project because it must be manually modified by the developer. If your new Objective-C class is to be used in Swift code, you need to edit the bridging header to add your Objective-C header file as an `import` statement as you would to use it with any other Objective-C file. Once the bridging header has been saved, the class is available to use in your Swift code. If you need to reference your Swift classes in the Objective-C classes you added to the project, the Swift bridging header is also available.

SYNTAX CHANGES

Swift does much of the hard work for you when you attempt to use Objective-C code outside its natural habitat, wrangling both syntax and types into a more Swift-native form during the import process.

Initializer names get particular attention: `init` and `initWith` are removed from the first portion of the initializer selector and the remainder is converted into the first parameter of the method. The remaining portions of the selector are converted into parameter values: For example `-initWithValue1:(Type1)value1 value2:(Type2)value2` becomes `init(value1:Type1, value2:Type2)`.

Class methods in Objective-C that behave as convenience initializers (like `+[MKObject objectWithValue:]`) are converted to regular initializers in Swift. The import process identifies that the class method begins with the same word as the class name, and the process is even smart enough to detect class prefixes in your class names and drop them when looking for matching convenience initializers.

Due to the larger number of potential variations in method names, the import process does not try to tidy them up in the same way it does with initializers. The first portion of the selector is used as the method name, and the remaining portions are converted into parameters.

If you rely on dot syntax in Objective-C as a way to retrieve a value from a method that takes no properties, be aware that you cannot do the same in Swift; you must call such methods using parentheses. The import process causes a strict separation of methods and properties.

TYPE CHANGES

The fundamental difference in type safety between Swift and Objective-C means that Objective-C classes need to be treated with a healthy degree of distrust when used from within Swift. Object instances passed to and from Objective-C methods are handled as optionals, albeit implicitly unwrapped optionals, on the Swift side. You're responsible for deciding if a value you're receiving from an Objective-C class can be safely used. If you wrote the class, and know that it always returns a value, you can use the implicitly unwrapped optional with confidence. If you don't know for sure that a class will not return `nil`, eye it with suspicion and use optional binding or chaining to ensure you don't encounter a runtime crash.

Objective-C methods that receive or return types such as `NSString`, `NSArray`, `NSDictionary`, or `NSNumber` are converted to use the corresponding native Swift types, as are C primitives like integers, floats, doubles, and Booleans.

The `id` type is converted to the Swift `AnyObject` protocol—you can call any method against an object that conforms to `AnyObject` because it has a neat little trick up its sleeve. Calling a method against `AnyObject` using optional chaining avoids a runtime error when the wrong type is assumed. Of course, using the type operators to determine what type of object you are actually working with is safer.

WORKING WITH C CODE

Objective-C without the C (or anything without the C) was a nice idea, but as long as you have the need to interoperate with Objective-C, you still need to occasionally work with C constructs. The developers of Swift have gone to great lengths to keep some of the "bare metal" aspects of C from Swift, but even interacting with Cocoa and Cocoa Touch APIs that rely on NSError to pass back error information to calling code requires some degree of interaction with pointers.

Swift comes with a small set of types created specifically for working with pointers. These can be used safely to interact with Objective-C APIs that rely on pointers. UnsafePointer, UnsafeMutablePointer, and AutoreleasingUnsafeMutablePointer are all generic types that can take a specific type (such as Int or Float) or Void to represent any type. Although it may not be apparent from the naming convention, they're also deemed to be unsafe; it's surprising that the developers of Swift didn't take advantage of Unicode and Emoji support to name them a bit more obvious: ⚠ Pointer?

Since it comes up so often, the case of NSError is worth examining. In the world of Objective-C, NSError is regularly used in the form of a pointer to an object pointer in method parameters, so that the method body can create a new NSError object and pass it back through the supplied pointer.

In the world of Swift, you can replicate this by passing an AutoreleasingUnsafeMutablePointer that is specifically typed as being a pointer to an optional NSError object. By passing an NSError? type variable as an in-out expression (achieved by prefixing with an &) to the API method, responsibility for the pointer itself can be handled by the Swift standard library.

```
var error: NSError?
let fileManager = NSFileManager.defaultManager()
fileManager.moveItemAtPath("sourcePath", toPath: "destPath", error: &error)
if let actualError = error {
    println(actualError.description)
}
```

Fortunately, most of your pointer interactions will likely be with older APIs that should hopefully be updated as adoption of Swift continues. Maybe before too long we can really have Objective-C without the C.

FRAMEWORKS

Swift and Objective-C code can be mixed and matched within any target type, which means you can create mixed source frameworks as well as applications. The frameworks can also be imported into any type of application target, regardless of the language it is written in.

When including Swift code in a framework, the most important thing to remember is the level of access control you give to your types. The default level of access control is `internal`; this is implied if you don't explicitly state a level, which means that your types are only visible within their own module or target. If you want to create an API that consumers of your framework can use, you need to mark the types you wish to access as `public`; you need to mark the methods and properties of those types `public` where you wish for them to be exposed as part of the API.

Although this may seem like a tedious extra step over the Objective-C equivalent, it does give an extra level of safety to your APIs. Without it, you would be resorting to the old Objective-C tricks of hiding methods in categories and manually migrating code between files to promote APIs from private to public—something achieved in Swift with a single keyword change.

WRAPPING UP

The developers of Swift have endeavored to make our adoption of Swift as smooth as any large-scale language transition can be. The ability to use both languages inside the same project or even within the same target will be an invaluable aid in speeding the migration process; the pains they have gone to in order to make Objective-C APIs appear as though they are native to Swift will help immensely.

We hope that this book helps you along the way as well.

May your transition journey be swift.

(Come on. Just one Swift pun in the whole book. Do you realize how much effort that took?)

INDEX

SYMBOLS

~ operator, 35
- operator, 32
-- operator, 32
.. operator, 35
/ operator, 32
|| operator, 32–33
| operator, 32
+ operator, 32
~= operator, 35
-= operator, 32
= operator, 32
== operator, 33
=== operator, 35
. operator, 33
! operator, 32–33, 35
% operator, 32
& operator, 32–34
* operator, 32
? operator, 33, 35
[ ] operator, 35
^ operator, 32
< operator, 32
> operator, 32
@ (at) sign, absence of, 27–28
{} (curly braces), requirement of, 42–43
( ) (parentheses)
   omission of, 29, 42
   using with functions, 66, 76–77
; (semicolon), absence of, 6, 27
[ ] (square) brackets, use of, 28

A

access control
   internal, 114
   private, 113
   public, 114
addition
   and assignment operator, 32
   operator, 32
   with overflow operator, 33
AnyObject primitive type, 21

Apple WWDC demo, downloading, 14
application delegate, using, 5–6
array contents, reading, 137–138
arrays, 24
   adding objects, 138–139
   creating, 137
   implementing, 144
   manipulating, 138–141
   modifying, 145
   removing objects from, 139–140
   replacing objects in, 140
   sorting, 141
   subscripting, 114
   Swift versus C, 136
as operator, 35
assertions, using in exception handling, 158
assignment operator, 32, 34
Assistant Editor, features of, 13
at (@) sign, absence of, 27–28

B

Balloons demo, downloading, 14
bit shift operator, 32
bitwise operator, 32
blocks. *See also* closures
   versus closures, 22
   creating references to, 83
   defining as parameters, 83–84
   inline creation of, 83
   passing into methods, 82
   receiving, 82
BOOL and Bool primitive types, 21
Boolean conditions, 43
bridging header, creating, 166

C

C arrays, 24
C code, working with, 170
C preprocessor, use of, 29
capture list, syntax for, 132

interactive documentation, use of, 14
iOS playground
    import statement, 11
    string variable, 11
is operator, 35

K

KVO (key-value observing), using in
    Objective-C, 158–159

L

Language pop-up menu, clicking, 4
lazy stored properties, using, 105–106
less-than comparisons, 32
let declaration, 24–25
logical operators, 32–33
long primitive types, 21
loops
    for and for-in, 44–45
    while and do-while, 45

M

main.m, absence of, 5
map function, using in Swift, 163
member access operator, 33
memory management
    object references, 130
    overview, 130
methods
    executing, 102
    versus functions, 102
    including in protocols, 148–150
    overriding, 111–112
    receiving blocks, 82
modules, importing, 5
multiplication operator, 32
multiply and ignore overflow operator, 33
mutability, 25–26
mutable arrays
    adding objects to, 138–139
    declaring, 144
mutating keyword, using with structures, 121

N

named parameters. *See also* parameters
    differentiated, 68–69
    matching, 68
namespaces, using in Swift, 160
nested functions. *See also* functions
    explained, 65
    using, 75–76
nested types, 126–127. *See also* enumerations;
    structures
nil coalescing operator, 63
nil objects, sending messages to, 61
None primitive type, 21
not equal operator, 33
NSError, using, 170
NSFastEnumeration protocol, counterpart to, 44
NSInteger primitive type, 21
NSString. *See also* strings
NSString
    comparing to Swift strings, 90
    conversions, 96
    creating explicitly, 96–97
    path modification, 96
    substrings, 95
    URL methods, 96
NSUInteger primitive type, 21

O

@objc attribute, using, 167
object methods, 102
object references, strong and weak, 130–131.
    See also reference types
object types, nesting, 23
Objective-C
    adding Swift files, 166
    dynamic dispatch, 159
    exception handling, 158
    KVO (key-value observing), 158–159
    reflection, 159
    using Swift code in, 167–168
Objective-C and Swift. *See also* Swift
    bridging header, 166
    C code, 170
    frameworks, 171
    syntax changes, 169
    type changes, 169
    using together, 6